REFLECTIONS
ON
HEAVEN AND HELL

REFLECTIONS ON HEAVEN AND HELL

Published and printed in the United States of America by
Fountain Publishing, P.O. Box 80011, Rochester, Michigan 48308

Cover painting by Frank S. Rose
Photographs by Frank S. Rose

Book design by Karin Alfelt Childs
Set in Palatino and Bernhard
ISBN 10: 1-936665-04-2
ISBN 13: 978-1-936665-04-4

Reflections

on

Heaven and Hell

FRANK S. ROSE

FOUNTAIN
PUBLISHING®
®

Dedicated to our son Charles,
born and died on August 7, 1964 —
the first of our family to experience life beyond the grave

Contents

Preface

Over two hundred fifty years ago, a remarkable book appeared in bookstores in England: *Heaven and Its Wonders and Hell, Drawn From Things Heard and Seen* by Emanuel Swedenborg (London, 1758). The book was published anonymously in Latin, the international language of the day. No one knew who the author was or even his nationality (Swedish).

Heaven and Hell, as the book is more commonly known, has remained in continuous print ever since. It has been translated into many languages and is the best known of Swedenborg's works.

Thirteen years before publishing *Heaven and Hell*, Swedenborg (1688-1772) began to have spiritual experiences that enabled him to go from a consciousness of this natural world to a consciousness of the spiritual world. Therefore, the full title of *Heaven and Hell* includes the words "from things heard and seen." Swedenborg wrote that he had visited both heaven and hell, and he described as best he could the remarkable order of things that he observed in the spiritual realm.

You are now about to read a series of my own reflections on some of the key concepts in Swedenborg's amazing book, further enhanced by my reading of observations by authors Raymond A. Moody Jr., M.D. and Wilson Van Dusen. *Heaven and Hell* has sixty-three chapters, and therefore I offer sixty-three small chapters of my own, discussing major points from each of Swedenborg's chapters. The reference numbers for the quotes at the beginning of each chapter refer to section numbers in *Heaven and Hell*, translated by George F. Dole. Bible quotes are drawn from the New King James Version. (See references, page 202.)

This book, *Reflections on Heaven and Hell*, is divided into three sections. The first, on heaven, consists of forty-three chapters. The opening chapters talk about the God of heaven and about heaven's basic structure. Later chapters deal with topics such as the language of angels, their homes, and their jobs.

The second section of this book is about the time and state between heaven and hell called "the world of spirits." This section contains twelve chapters concerning how a person wakes up in the spiritual world and goes through various stages leading to that person's ultimate destination. Section two ends with an encouraging chapter discussing the fact that leading a heaven-bound life is not as difficult as people might think.

The last section of this book is the shortest and deals with the grim prospect of hell. Note that hell is not a punishment, and people in hell are free to leave whenever they want. The eight chapters of this section give a new perspective on such things as hellfire and help us to understand the nature of evil.

My hope is that this book will provide a gentle introduction to some of the key concepts from Swedenborg's *Heaven and Hell*, and will also share my thoughts about how life in the spiritual world relates to our lives on earth.

Frank S. Rose
Tucson, Arizona

Heaven

"First and foremost, we need to know who the God of heaven is, since everything else depends on this. Throughout the whole of heaven, no one is acknowledged as God of heaven except the Lord."

HEAVEN AND HELL 2

CHAPTER 1

Who Is the God of Heaven?

One of the first things to strike Emanuel Swedenborg in his spiritual journeys was that wherever he went in heaven, only one God was acknowledged and worshiped, and that God was the Lord Jesus Christ. This observation fits in with the words at the end of the Gospel of Matthew, where Jesus says: "All authority has been given to me in heaven and on earth." (Matthew 28:18) The first chapter of *Heaven and Hell* announces that the God of heaven is the Lord.

Swedenborg believed that there is really only one God, though that God might be known by many different names. When Swedenborg wrote that Jesus, or "the Lord," is that God, he was saying that when Jesus rose in glory he became "one with the Father." Jesus was the manifestation in human form of that Great Spirit, Allah, the Almighty, worshiped in all religions.

The government of heaven is the government of love. It is also infinitely wise and has a human face. Jesus said that we need to "abide in him and he in us" (John 15:4) the way branches are connected to the vine. He even said that he went to prepare a place in heaven for us (John 14:1), "that where I am, there you may be also." (John 14:3) Many people think of heaven in terms of being "with Jesus" for that reason. Swedenborg confirms that the Lord Jesus Christ is the God of heaven.

"While we call the total assemblage of angels heaven because they do make it up, what really makes heaven overall and in every specific instance is the divine nature that emanates from the Lord, flowing into angels and accepted by them."

HEAVEN AND HELL 7

Chapter 2
What Makes Heaven?

A woman was talking about her favorite school, and said, "Of course, it's not the buildings or the organizational structure that make the school—it's the people."

Her friend asked, "What is it about the people that you like so much?"

The woman replied, "It's their dedication to their work and to their students. It's their spirit of compassion and integrity. This is a fine group of people. That's what the school is to me."

This view is true of all human organizations. What we like or dislike about them is the people and their attitudes. If we were to visit a society of angels, we would be deeply impressed by the people, that is, the angels. We might even say, "Now I know why heaven is such a delightful place. You angels are wonderful. I love your spirit of kindness, your intelligence, your devotion. I love everything about you."

The angels might respond: "Don't give us the credit. What you are noticing is the Lord's spirit that works in us and through us. The divine life fills our hearts with love, and so we are compassionate and kind. The divine light fills our minds, and so we have intelligence and wisdom. The divine energy moves us to act, and so we are useful. Without these divine qualities flowing into us, we would be nothing. We merely receive these qualities. What makes heaven is not something special about us but the Lord's own life flowing into us."

A beautiful painting consists of dabs of paint on a surface. These dabs become a work of art when organized by the artist. It is the vision, emotions and thoughts of the artist that make the painting. The dabs of paint merely constitute it. One way of looking at what the angels in our example were saying is that God is the artist and the angels are the dabs of paint. The angels are organized into something beautiful, but it is God who is the life behind that beauty.

God is love, and love is the connecting force that makes heaven the wonderful place that it is. Love is the essential life of every person, because love is also the essence of God. When the divine love fills the heart of an angel, the angel is said to be "in heaven" because heaven is in the angel. In other words, heaven is heaven because of the people there, and those people—the angels—receive all their wonderful qualities straight from God's love.

*"All the people [in heaven]
are forms of love and thoughtfulness."*
HEAVEN AND HELL 17

CHAPTER 3

How the Lord's Qualities Are Received by Angels

I once knew a person who had all of the elements of failure in his life. He was not particularly good-looking. He was physically weak. Because of severe health problems, there were very few jobs he could do. And he was poor. He was also one of the most loving people I have ever known. People were drawn to him. In his presence they felt accepted. He did not give advice, but those who talked to him about their problems went away with more confidence in handling them. He had a glow about him that made him a delightful person to be with. I often thought that being with him was like being with an angel.

There have been other people in my life with that quality. Some were autistic or had Down syndrome. Many were children.

I have sometimes wondered what life would be like if every person we met had that same open and loving quality, and I have concluded that it would be heaven. To live among angels must bring a sense of total acceptance.

It is different dealing with people who are so full of themselves that, when they are talking with me, I feel as if the person I am is invisible to them. It feels as if they are just trying to use me for their own ends.

In a way you could say that every person in the world is looking for happiness. Some look for it in things or in pleasures. Then there are those who don't seem to be looking for it at all, because their focus is more on what they give than on what they expect to receive.

A mindset that focuses more on giving than on receiving is similar to the mindset of angels. Angels have allowed themselves to be filled up with God's divine love, and so they also absorb all of the qualities that go along with that love. Angels in heaven or people on earth who care for other people and radiate love for them are blessed with a special kind of intelligence, wisdom, peace and happiness. In short, heaven is in them, and they are in heaven.

"Since there are infinite varieties in heaven—since no community and in fact no individual is just like any other—heaven is therefore divided overall, more specifically, and in detail."

HEAVEN AND HELL 20

CHAPTER 4

The Head and the Heart: Two Important Parts of the Whole

Two people lived in the same small town. One was a professor. She was very intellectual, had an intense love of reading, and analyzed every situation. People thought of her as cool, even lacking in emotion. But she was not that way at all. She did not wear her emotions on her sleeve. She cared intensely about the things she was learning and teaching, and also about her students. The students were a little bit afraid of her and at times thought that she was not particularly interested in them as people. But long after they had graduated from school, they looked back on her as one of the most caring teachers they'd ever had and the one they admired the most.

Living in the same town was a man who, though he was smart, was not much of a reader. What little he did read would go into his mind and, if he believed it to be true, directly into his behavior. The principles he believed in were the same principles that he lived by. He was very active in the community, gardening, building things, visiting friends who did not get out much, and generally touching the lives of many others. When talking with someone else he usually had his hand on their shoulder and a smile on his face, and he seemed completely absorbed in what they were saying. He was very affectionate and at the same time very practical in the things he did for other people to show that he cared.

These two individuals, the professor and the gardener, were as different as the head and the heart. Though their paths did not cross very often and they did not have a personal relationship, they knew about each other and respected each other. They knew that they both were an important part of the whole community.

In heaven and on earth, all kinds of people are needed to make up complete communities and a complete spiritual or natural world. Some people will operate more from the head and some more from the heart. God values and uses both kinds of people to do his work.

*"It is the inner nature of angels
that determines which heaven they are in."*

HEAVEN AND HELL 33

CHAPTER 5

The Levels of Heaven

It is fascinating to watch look-alike competitions. A parade of people appear on the stage, and judges are there to see which one looks most like some famous person. As I watch the contestants, it strikes me how little they look like each other and how none of them really looks like the famous person.

One of the most fascinating things about life is the endless variety of faces in this world. Considering the fact that the human face consists of very few basic elements (eyes, nose, mouth, chin, etc.), you might think that we would all look pretty much the same. But we are all totally different, and there never will be two faces that are completely identical, even with so-called "identical twins." And that is just comparing one physical aspect of a person—what his or her face looks like! Looking more deeply, the minds of people are even more strikingly different.

There is only one Life in the universe, and that Life is infinite. Each human being receives that one Life in a special way.

As noted in chapter 4, we can generalize and say that some people are more into their feelings while others are more into their thoughts. Some people are deep thinkers. Others are much more interested in action.

It is no wonder that heaven is varied, consisting as it does of angels, each of whom receives life in a unique way. There are levels of heaven, because some of the angels receive the life of God more deeply than others.

In general there are angels who are very much in touch with the love of God and who open their hearts fully to that love. Other angels are more concerned about their love for other people. Still others are most interested in living a good moral and practical life. These three approaches make up the three main levels of heaven.

The highest level is called "heavenly" (or "celestial") and consists of angels whose main love is love to the Lord.

The second level is called "spiritual," and the angels there are primarily in the love of other people.

The third and lowest level is called "natural," and the angels on that level live a good moral life.

Angels in the different heavens are invisible to each other. When you look at the various human groupings in a typical large city, you find the same thing. There are people whose lives revolve around sports. Others are into business and high finance. Still others are doing jobs of very little interest to them, and they divert themselves by watching endless hours of television. Then there are those who know every local band and music group, and love to spend time going to listen to them. There are bird-watchers, artists, stamp collectors, people who go to garage sales, gamblers, and so on and on. It would be practically impossible to list all of the groups and subgroups in a large city. And most of us are aware only of the people in a few of these groups. The others are virtually invisible to us. And yet somehow they all make one city, just as all of the various levels and societies of heaven make one. God is the unifying element in all these various groups and levels of life. Out of this enormous variety and these many levels, God creates one single entity—the realm of God.

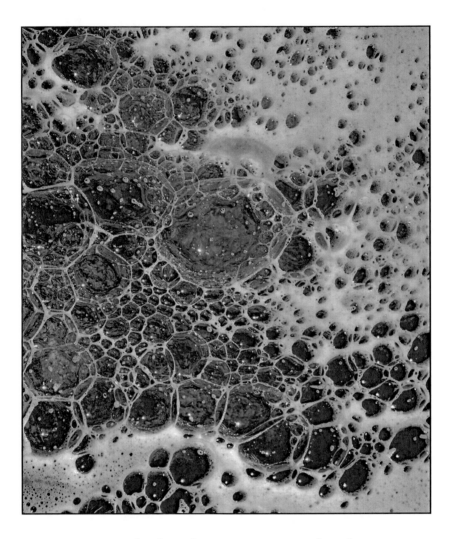

"Kindred souls gravitate toward each other spontaneously, as it were, for with each other they feel as though they are with their own family, at home."

HEAVEN AND HELL 44

CHAPTER 6

The Communities of Heaven

Two people were talking about the frustration of having family and friends so widely separated in this world.

"I hate having our family so scattered," said one person. "The older ones have moved south, the young ones are in the growing cities, and the grandparents still live in the old country. I wish we could all be together."

"Well, at least when we die and go to heaven we will all be together," said the other.

"No, we won't. We might be even farther apart there than we are here!" That startling thought more or less ended the conversation.

In this world, time and space determine whether people are together or not. To be with each other they have to be in the same place at the same time. But after death "time is no more," and neither is space. Rather, time and space are spiritual qualities, and people are together if they are spiritually similar. If the things they are interested in are vastly different, they will not be in the same part of heaven.

Heaven does not consist of one vast, endless expanse. The angels live in communities, some large, some small, much as we do on earth. The difference is that angelic communities consist of people who are spiritually close to each other, not those who are physically close. Furthermore, because angels are similar in their thoughts and feelings, they even look something like each other. This phenomenon exists to a certain extent even on this earthly plane. People often settle somewhere because they feel in some way similar to other people settled in that area. Even in the vast metropolitan areas there are cluster communities, united by various factors such as ethnic origin, social class, occupation, wealth and so on.

Swedenborg observed that when people enter their heavenly community for the first time, they feel totally at home, and when they meet people there, it is as if they have always known and loved those people. The people entering the community have "come home" to live with others who share similar interests, similar affections, and a similar life view.

Does this mean that heavenly communities are uniform? Not at all. Within each community there is still plenty of room for variety—enough variety, in fact, for each community to be like a miniature of the whole of heaven.

The Lord's life flows into every community of heaven and is received differently by each one. Since there is only one life flowing in, all these different heavenly towns, villages and cities communicate with each other and are combined into a perfect harmony, like one great organic whole. The Lord guides the angels to the places, the groups, and the useful actions that will best bring out their love and their wisdom, and therefore the most happiness.

"Heaven is not outside angels but within them."

HEAVEN AND HELL 53

CHAPTER 7

The Human Form of Heaven

What do angels look like? They look just like people on earth, only more beautiful.

The reason our physical bodies are the way they are is so that we can function in the world. Why would angels need eyes? They don't live in the light of the natural sun. This is true, and therefore angels don't have physical or material eyes. They have spiritual eyes.

What are spiritual eyes?

Spiritual eyes are the part of the mind that "sees" or understands. Every part of the body has some counterpart in the mind. People speak of having a "backbone" (when they mean having courage), of not being able to "digest" an idea, of "smelling" a rat, and so on. The body is an image of the mind. The many organs of the body are like the many faculties of the mind. Indeed there is no part of the human body that does not have some corresponding part in the spirit.

Heaven is organized as one big human form, with all the many communities acting as the various organs. Each angel is also in human form with the many components of the angel's mind taking form as the body of the angel. Therefore angels look like people. The difference is that angels are seen, not in the light of the world, but in the light of heaven, and not with the eyes of the body, but with the eyes of the spirit.

"Angels never pay attention to what someone's body is doing, but rather to the intent from which the body is acting."

HEAVEN AND HELL 61

CHAPTER 8

The Whole of Heaven Resembles a Single Person

In a fascinating way, every community of heaven is also in a human form. We even talk about the nerves and arteries of a city. We talk about its heart. A city has an infrastructure, just as a human body has an infastructure of bones and sinews.

Just as the parts in a human body are performing a series of functions to keep that body going, there is also a network of functions in any community, whether in heaven or on earth. Small towns and villages have relatively simple systems—one school, a couple of supermarkets, maybe a bank, a post office and so on. As a town grows, so does the complexity of its systems. Large cities can have a tremendous choice of stores, schools, entertainment centers, legal offices, clubs and activities.

The communities or societies of heaven are similar. Some operate much like our smaller towns and villages, and some like our large cities. Parts of a human body function best when there are plenty of healthy, working cells, and heavenly communities function best when there are plenty of angels. Therefore, angels love nothing more than having new members—new angels— come to join them. On earth larger numbers may improve a city or increase its chaos, depending on how well-ordered the city is and how well the people conduct themselves. In heaven, where all who arrive in new communities are eager to contribute, larger numbers can only increase the perfection of the community.

As mentioned before, the whole of heaven is like a single human organism, with each community of heaven making its own unique contribution. The angels even know what part of this grand, organic whole they serve. Some are in the province of the eye, belonging to a community that helps others to "see" or understand. Some are in the province of the lips, and so on.

This whole incredibly complex organism works on a grand scale like a single human being does on a small scale. The angels, with all their various communities and functions, combine to form the body of one grand human being. The Lord is the soul of that grand human being, because he is the one who flows into every part with his love and his wisdom and gives it life.

*"Angels long for nothing more
than to have new angel guests arrive."*

HEAVEN AND HELL 71

CHAPTER 9

The Body of Christ

I was once watching a partial eclipse of the sun. Standing in the shade of a tree, I looked at the dappled light filtering through the gaps in the leaves. Normally this set-up would result in a pattern of circles projected onto the ground. Because the sun was no longer a circle, but moon-shaped, the ground was covered with moons, each one projected through spaces between the leaves as an image of the sun. As the eclipse went through its phases, so did these little patterns of light, until, at the end of the eclipse, they were all perfect circles again. This is one of nature's most dramatic examples of how the sun projects pictures of itself onto the earth.

As my wife and I have gone out hiking recently, we have seen the desert burst into bloom. Everywhere we see golden flowers, like a million miniature suns capturing a small part of the glory of the original. In springtime it seems as if the sun, through wildflowers, is creating thousands of different images of itself.

Swedenborg writes that the sun symbolizes God and also that God is human. We can find images of the sun in nature, and on a more complex level, we can also see something of the human form in all of creation.

Most animals have some kind of brain, sensory organs, digestive systems, hearts, lungs, muscles, and even shapes that are similar to the human form. In the plant kingdom, too, there are systems that mirror human systems. Even in groups of human beings—communities—there are people who tend to make up the "brains" of each group, or the heart or the digestive system or the nervous system. Swedenborg describes the whole of heaven as being in the form of a human being. Different angels and angel communities make up the various systems that complement each other and work together. Heaven, as a whole, reflects the human form of God, and each individual person or angel reflects the human form of heaven.

Christ said that people should abide in him and he in them. (John 15:4) Following this idea, early Christians took to calling the Church the "body of Christ." Paul reminded them that the various parts of the body are all different, and yet are all important parts of the whole. Paul pointed out to his listeners that they all belonged to the same system, and so they should not see their differences as a cause for finding fault with others.

> There are many members, yet one body. And the eye cannot say to the hand, "I have no need of you"; nor again the head to the feet, "I have no need of you." (1 Corinthians 12:20-21)

Paul reminded his listeners that

> If one member suffers, all the members suffer with it; or if one member is honored, all the members rejoice with it. Now you are the body of Christ, and members individually. (1 Corinthians 12:26,27)

This concept of the early Christian community being the body of Christ is an amazing one, especially when we compare it to the idea that the whole of heaven is organized into a system of useful functions that mirror the functions in the human body. The divine essence of the Lord is the soul of heaven, and angels are the cells, enlivened by that soul, which make up the body. Communities of angels form the organs of that body. God, the soul of heaven, is "human," and is the essential human form which creates us in God's image and likeness. We are human because God, our source and creator, is human.

> Every community in heaven is growing in numbers daily, and the more it grows, the more perfect it becomes. In this way, not only is the community perfected, but heaven in general is perfected as well, since the communities constitute heaven. Since heaven is perfected by its numerical growth, we can see how mistaken people are who believe that heaven will be closed to prevent overcrowding. Actually, it is just the reverse. It will never be closed, and its ever increasing fullness makes it more perfect. So angels long for nothing more than to have new angel guests arrive there. (*Heaven and Hell* 71)

Incredibly, not only are human individuals created in the

image and likeness of God; groups of humans, too, are created in that image and likeness, including the whole group of angels that make up heaven. Jesus Christ as he rose in glory on Easter is that divine human God which is the soul of heaven, and it is really true that we live in him and he in us.

"*We cannot see angels with our bodily eyes,
only with the eyes of our spirit.*"

HEAVEN AND HELL 76

CHAPTER 10

Every Angel Is in a Perfect Human Form

There were many television shows and movies that my family and I missed in earlier years. This was partly because we were living outside the United States, but mostly because in those days we had very little time for watching television. Now we are able to look at some of the shows, including some involving space travel and some involving spirits and angels. I find it fascinating that, in most cases, these alien or spiritual beings are recognizably human.

There are many Bible stories involving angels, and the angels are in human forms. King Saul saw his former spiritual leader, Samuel, and recognized him, even though Samuel had died some time before. Jesus' disciples saw Moses and Elijah talking with Jesus in the vision on the mountain. In some cases angels are mistaken for human beings on earth until they vanish or do something that shows they are not still on this plane. Also, Paul talks of us rising after death with a spiritual body, to all appearances like the body we left behind.

People who have had near-death experiences report seeing people they have known, as well as angels. The people look enough like they did on earth that they are easy to recognize. They and other angels are all seen in human forms.

Swedenborg writes that people in this world and the next all appear in human forms. The angels may be more perfect than we are. They may radiate light. But they are not so different as to make us wonder what they are. Angels can see each other, because they have eyes. They can hear each other and converse, because they have ears and mouths. They have hands to grasp things and feet to walk with.

After death we will not be formless bits of thought or energy. We will still be in human forms, only in more perfect human forms.

"Angels say that they are 'in the Lord' and even
that they are 'in his body,' meaning that they are in
the very substance of his love."

HEAVEN AND HELL 81

CHAPTER 11

God Is the Original Human and the Source of All That Is Human

The Bible tells the story of a man named Gideon (Judges 6). He was distressed, because he and his fellow Israelites seemed to be powerless against their enemies. He was threshing wheat when an angel of the Lord came and sat down under an oak tree. At first it seems as if just an angel is talking to Gideon. Then, a few verses later, it is the Lord speaking to him. Compare this story with the story of Abraham seeing a stranger, then realizing that the stranger is the Lord. In these and other places, it is clear that, at the rare times when God appeared to people in the stories of the Bible, he appeared in angelic form, and the angelic form is the human form.

When we think of a person we might think in terms of physical appearance, but after a while we think more of that person's spirit, and his or her qualities of caring and understanding. Those and other such qualities are what make a person truly human. We can relate to other humans, because we all share the ability to think, love and communicate.

In most cultures, God is pictured in some kind of human or human-like form. This may be because God has our human qualities in infinite measure. We can love on a limited scale. God can love totally and completely. We can understand a few things. God is all-knowing. We are human, because God is the original human form. The Bible says that we, men and women, were created in God's image and likeness.

"After death, our spirit looks the way it actually did within the body while we were living in it in this world."

HEAVEN AND HELL 99

CHAPTER 12

Spiritual Things Have Parallels in Nature

When people look at beautiful and remarkable things in nature, they have a sense that they are seeing something beyond the physical plane. It is as if the whole of nature, with its forms and processes, is like a theater in which heaven is presented to us.

Swedenborg writes about the concept of "correspondences." This term refers to the idea that there is a direct relationship between spiritual realities and physical items on earth. Every item in nature, for instance, presents a physical picture of something about God or of something in our minds.

Nature imagery appears frequently in the Bible. The first Psalm compares a good person to a "tree planted by the rivers of water." (Psalm 1:3) According to Swedenborg's concept of correspondences, "the rivers" symbolize the river of life, consisting not of water but of the truth that flows out from God. The "tree" symbolizes a person, with its leaves presenting a picture of true ideas in a person's mind. The fruit symbolizes the good and kind things done by a person as an expression of faith; Jesus confirmed this idea when he said that a "tree is known by its fruits." (Matthew 12:33) The structure and life of a tree correspond to the spiritual life of a person. This is an example of a process in nature that presents a picture of a development of the mind and spirit.

There are many other examples of such correspondences. Some of them are so common that people take them for granted, like the transformation from a caterpillar to a butterfly as presenting a picture of two phases of human life, the natural and the spiritual. Imagine looking at any mineral, plant, animal, fish or bird and thinking that its form provides us with a picture of something of heaven!

"Not one thing of beauty and delight ever exists in the sky above or on earth beneath that is not in some respect representative of the Lord's kingdom." (*Secrets of Heaven* 1807:2, my translation)

"When we are absorbed in the knowledge of correspondences we can be in the company of angels in respect to the thoughts of our minds." (*Heaven and Hell* 114)

The world of nature provides a beautiful way to see and learn things about heaven.

*"Absolutely everything in nature,
from the smallest to the greatest,
is a correspondence."*

HEAVEN AND HELL 106

CHAPTER 13

Everything on Earth Corresponds to Something in Heaven

There is something very healing about going out into nature. Many times I have hiked in the mountains, often coming to some area with a magnificent view. Two hours of hiking might culminate in a few minutes of taking in the beauty of my surroundings. It has seemed to me that such mountain-top moments are a permanent gift to my soul. Why should this be? Perhaps it is just the deep impression left on our minds and hearts by panoramic vistas. It is also possible that the forms of nature, while beautiful in themselves, tell us of even deeper wonders.

Swedenborg beautifully describes a reason for these powerful feelings in *Secrets of Heaven* (also known as *Arcana Coelestia*).

> When people who see deeper meaning in external things look at the sky, they do not think at all of the starry sky but of the angelic heaven. And when they see the sun, they do not think about the sun but about the Lord's being the sun of heaven. The same applies when they see the moon and also the stars. And so when they see the vastness of the sky, they do not think about its vastness but about the Lord's boundless and infinite power. The same holds true for everything else they see, for there is nothing that is not representative.
>
> It is the same with the things belonging to the earth. When, for example, such people see the dawning of the day, they do not think of the dawn but of the rise of all things from the Lord and of advancement into the daylight of wisdom. Similarly when they see cultivated gardens, trees, and flowers, their eye is not fixed on any tree and on its blossom, leaf, and fruit, but on the heavenly things which these represent. Nor is the eye fixed on any flower and its beauty and loveliness but on those things which these represent in the next life. For nothing beautiful and delightful ever exists in the sky above or on earth beneath that is not in some measure representative of the Lord's realm. (*Secrets of Heaven* 1807, my translation)

Or, as Shakespeare put it,

And this our life, exempt from public haunt,
Finds tongues in trees, books in the running brooks,
Sermons in stones, and good in everything.
I would not change it . . . .[1]

"Since the Lord does appear in heaven as a sun because of the divine love that is in him and from him, all the people there constantly turn toward him."

HEAVEN AND HELL 123

CHAPTER 14

The Spiritual Sun and Its Heat

As my wife and I hike through the desert we come across all kinds of vegetation: the giant saguaro, the tiny pincushion cacti, the flame-tipped ocotillo, the round pads of the prickly pear, and, in the Spring, a host of beautiful desert flowers. The California poppies wait until the sun is full in the sky before opening as if in worship. It seems that all plants are conscious of the sun. On those rare overcast days, you can always know which way is south by the great barrel cactus. In this desert the sun hangs in the southwestern part of the sky, and as the barrel cacti grow they lean in a southerly direction in response to that sunlight.

Of course all plants depend on the heat and light of the sun for their survival, and so do all living things. When Swedenborg was given the privilege of visiting the spiritual world even while living on earth, he noticed that there is heat and light in heaven and also that there is a source of that heat and light. This source is not some atomic furnace of physical fire millions of miles away, but rather the source is a different golden disc in the heavenly sky, similar to our sun in appearance but consisting of a totally different essence—the essence of spiritual fire, which is love.

We know that heat is related to love, as when we talk of a "heartwarming" experience or being "all fired up." We also talk about light and darkness when referring to the mind, as when we say "I was in the dark about that," or "I thought about it for a long time, and then a light went on in my head."

In heaven the angels feel the warmth of the spiritual sun, and they see by its light. And what is that sun? That sun is the Lord! The New Testament describes a time when a few of the disciples saw the Lord transfigured. "His face shone like the sun, and his clothes became as white as the light." (Matthew 17:2)

The heat and light that come from the spiritual sun are the divine love and the divine truth that radiate from the Lord. Just as our physical life depends on the energy that comes from the sun, so too our spiritual life depends on the sun, but it is the sun of heaven, or the Lord.

When the Lord appears *in* heaven [as opposed to appearing

as a sun above heaven] (which happens quite often) he does not appear clothed with the sun but in angelic form, distinguishable from the angels by the divine quality that shines from his face . . . . Then too I have seen the Lord outside the sun in an angelic form overhead, a little below the sun, and also nearby in a similar form—once even among some angels, looking like a fiery ray of light. (*Heaven and Hell* 121)

*"People are recognized in heaven's light
for what they really are."*

HEAVEN AND HELL 131

CHAPTER 15

Light and Warmth in Heaven

Some people who come very near the point of death and recover describe having the amazing experience of waking up into a new world. Most of them describe seeing a light of indescribable brilliance which yet did not hurt their eyes, this at a time when their physical eyes were closed. They also talk about understanding things in that light that they had not understood before. Examples like these appear in books such as *Life After Life* by Dr. Raymond Moody. Evidently these people were seeing with the eyes of the spirit, or the mind, and the light must have been spiritual, not natural.

Physical light is amazing, and is a vital part of life. And what is spiritual light? It is the light that turns on in the mind when we see some concept for the first time, the light of understanding. Throughout the Bible, light is used with that spiritual meaning.

Warmth is so clearly related to love that it is incorporated into our everyday speech. We talk of people as being warm or cold. We talk of someone's ranting as having more heat than light. We experience warmth in our hearts when we are affected by love.

Isn't it fascinating to think that we already deal with these two very different kinds of light and heat, physical and spiritual? Even on earth we are living in two different worlds—the physical world, and the world of the mind and heart. Each world has its own light and warmth.

"Angels turn and direct their faces and bodies in any direction just as we do, but still, the east is always before their eyes."

Heaven and Hell 143

CHAPTER 16

Directions in Heaven

A man was talking to his son. The mood was tense. The father was convinced that his boy was going in a bad direction. "Son," he said, "you need to do a one-eighty." The son knew exactly what the father meant. A full circle is 360 degrees, so a "180" is half a circle. In effect the son knew he was being told that he had to turn his life around completely.

The example above provides a little lesson in spiritual geography. Just as the surface of the earth is divided into various regions and zones, so are there different areas in the world that our spirits live in. Some of these spiritual regions are beautiful, and others are extremely dangerous. Spiritual growth involves going through different landscapes of this spiritual world. Children start out in a kind of paradise—"eastward in Eden." As they grow up they lose much of that childhood innocence and begin exploring worlds opened up to them through education and experience. This exploration is like a journey to the south, because the direction "south" corresponds to wisdom and intelligence (see *Heaven and Hell* 150).

When people have a spiritual awakening in their adult years, they might find themselves far from the kind of spiritual place they want to be in, and so they begin to try to orient themselves. This spiritual journey often requires a new direction. Such people want to know where to look for the source of their growth. They journey back to the east, because that direction corresponds to a clear perception of love and goodness. In childhood we dwell in an innocent perception of love and goodness. In adulthood we must choose to journey to a wise perception of love and goodness.

When we talk of "orienting ourselves," we are using the word for the east (the Orient). Though the Lord is present in all of heaven, he is seen as the spiritual sun in the east, the direction of the rising sun. The spiritual sun provides a picture of the Lord as the source of all life, and so Swedenborg describes the angels as constantly facing the east. This description seems strange, and yet "facing east" is another way of saying that, whatever the angels are doing, they are always looking to the Lord, their source. Spiritually speaking, no matter what direction the angels turn, they are always facing east.

It is useful to stop and ask ourselves how we feel about where we are spiritually. What is our spiritual geography like? Where should we turn if we want to find a better spiritual place? If we determine our destination to be the Lord and a growing perception of his love, then we can better plan a journey in which we will head in that direction.

> The reason they give the name "east" to the direction in which the Lord is seen as the sun is that the whole *source* of life is from him as the sun. Further, to the extent that warmth and light, or intelligence and wisdom from him, are accepted among angels, they say that the Lord has *risen* among them. This is also why the Lord is called the east in the Word. (*Heaven and Hell* 141)

"*Each individual angel undergoes and passes through changes of state . . . and so too does each community collectively.*"

HEAVEN AND HELL 157

CHAPTER 17

Angels Experience Change in Heaven

Normally I meditate with my two hands in my lap, palms up, with my little fingers just touching. On one occasion, as I was coming out of the meditation, I began to wonder if the fingers were touching or not. With my eyes closed, I could not tell. The only ways to answer the question were to move my fingers or to open my eyes. This little experience reminded me that the sense of touch, like all other senses, depends on motion. If the sound waves were not vibrating, we would not hear. If light did not travel in waves, we would not see. And if we touch something long enough without moving, we no longer feel. Change is essential to sensation.

But you hear people say that they do not like change. Some people even look forward to leaving the physical plane so that they can live in a world that is not so much in flux. "Oh to be in heaven, where things are static and unchanging!"

It has been said that the only thing that is constant in the world is change. Without change there is no motion, no growth, no progress, and thus no life! We need change and could not live without it. We go through various mood shifts. We might have a moment of high inspiration and might hope that we will never come down to earth again. Try as we may, we cannot make that period of bliss last forever. Like the times of day and the seasons of the year, our inner world has rhythms and cycles. Far from being a problem, these changes are essential.

When two forces are working in opposite directions, there is likely to be change, and on earth we are living a life between two forces. Spiritually we are powerfully influenced by the unselfish love of God flowing into us from above and lifting us up, and at the same time we are pulled down by our own inertia and tendency to be selfish. Between these two forces there is a constant flux. At one moment the divine love lifts us up out of ourselves to experience love and joy on a very high plane. We cannot stay at this height forever, and something of self draws us back down to the physical and the personal. After a while we grow restless in this self-centeredness and we open ourselves to the elevating power of God. And so the cycle continues, pulling us ever forward into new stages of growth.

In heaven angels are no longer plagued with the kind of self-ish tendencies we deal with on earth. And yet angels still experience change. There are many reasons why change is still necessary for life, even in heaven. First, life would become dull and unpleasant for the angels if there was no variety. Second, even though angels are no longer selfish, they still carry with them a sense of self and a love of self. They experience fluctuations between being caught up in themselves and being caught up in knowing that everything good in them is from the Lord. A third reason is that it is only by going through these fluctuations and changes that angels keep learning new things and becoming more perfect.

Both on earth and in heaven, change is something that allows life to flow and allows growth and progress to take place.

"Even though things keep happening in sequence and progressing in heaven the way they do in the world, still angels have no notion or concept of time and space."

HEAVEN AND HELL 162

CHAPTER 18

Time in Heaven

Wouldn't it be nice if we did not have to live with the limitations of space and time! Sometimes it seems as if space and time are two big enemies. Concerning time, how often do we hear people say: "There are not enough hours in the day," "I just haven't got time," and even, "I have too much time—it's driving me crazy."

What would life be like without these limitations? The answer is simple. It would be heaven! When people pass from this world to the next, they leave behind all concerns about the limitations of earthly life. There are no clocks or calendars in heaven. But the lack of time-measuring devices does not mean that eternal life is always the same.

Life in the spiritual world is constantly changing. It has a flow and a direction to it, the way time does in this world, but life in the spiritual world is not measured. The angels simply go through the various phases of their life corresponding to our morning, afternoon and evening without having to be told by the clock what to do when.

Imagine what your life would be like if you just finished whatever you were doing and then went on to do the next thing, not because the clock told you to, but because you were ready. This is what heaven is like. Many people enjoy retirement because it has a similar quality. It is interesting how our vacation time and our time off begin to imitate the time of heaven, which is just a natural flow from one state of mind to another, and from one activity to another.

As we grow spiritually we learn how to honor the fact that our spirits, even as we live in this world, operate beyond the time-space framework. And it is interesting to note that many human inventions are designed to make this world more like the spiritual world by overcoming, at least to some extent, the limitations of space and time.

"Things that arise from heaven's sun are called spiritual, while things that arise from our world's sun are called natural."

HEAVEN AND HELL 172

CHAPTER 19

What Will We See Around Us in Heaven?

Heaven is a state of mind, which is why Jesus said "the kingdom of God is within you." (Luke 17:21) And yet Swedenborg's descriptions and many accounts of near-death experiences tell us that in heaven we will see beautiful surroundings. There are trees, flowers, fields, streams, mountains, sky, sun, moon and stars. There are homes, and the homes contain furniture and works of art. In short, the spiritual world looks a lot like the natural world. And so what is the difference between the two?

The main difference is that the things seen in heaven are the result of the inner lives of the angels. According to Swedenborg, the surroundings in heaven come into being "from the Lord in response to the deeper natures of the angels." (*Heaven and Hell* 173) The homes of angels are a reflection of their loves and thoughts. The scenery around them expresses the quality of their inner world.

We do not often experience this perfect harmony with our environment in the natural world. There are times when our spirits are bright, and the weather is dull and dreary. At other times the weather is cheerful, but we are not. Beautiful things can happen in very ordinary surroundings in this world, and ugliness can exist inside a person whose material possessions are beautiful. This lack of harmony can give this planet an unreal feeling at times. In heaven, where the things around the angels correspond perfectly with the thoughts and feelings within them, life is always in harmony.

The faces of angels are perfect expressions of their inner selves. The decorations in their homes tell a story about the quality of their wisdom and love. Therefore the spiritual world feels more real to the angels than our natural world feels to us.

Of course we can strive to make our external world correspond to the world inside us. We can work to make our life on earth approximate the life of heaven. We begin by striving for unselfish love of others, inner harmony and peace. And then we do what we can to express those spiritual qualities in the world around us.

*"The clothes angels wear . . . . reflect their
intelligence, so all the people in heaven are
dressed according to their intelligence."*

HEAVEN AND HELL 178

CHAPTER 20

Angelic Clothing

I grew up in the Depression years, and most of our clothes were hand-me downs from older siblings, who, in turn, probably had many of those clothes handed down from classmates in richer families. Ever since then it has been hard for me to take fashion seriously. With others I enjoy having a laugh at fashions of the twenties (the very same years of my early childhood) and wondering how people in the future will keep from splitting their sides when they see what we consider the height of fashion today. It will be a relief to go to the spiritual world, where clothing still exists, but where it comes from the quality of the wearer's mind, not from the dictates of contemporary trends.

I remember hearing a speech in my high school years on "the well-dressed feminine mind," given by a teacher in an all-girls high school. The phrase has stayed with me as I have come to know people, both men and women, and have considered the wonderful ideas and thoughts that adorn their minds.

In the Bible we find that when the dress of angels is mentioned, it is usually white, an impractical color in biblical times. The impression given is not one of fashion, but of the brilliance and purity of innocent wisdom.

As our thoughts change depending on our moods, it is easy to see how the dress of angels varies in color and brightness according to the changing states of mind that they go through. In any case I can imagine that someone seeing an angel would not have to think "Why is she wearing that?" but rather could wonder "What wonderful thought processes express themselves in such a beautiful garment?"

"The houses angels live in are not constructed as houses in our world are, but are given them by the Lord gratis, to each individual according to his or her acceptance of what is good and true."

HEAVEN AND HELL 190

CHAPTER 21

Angelic Homes

There are a few really basic human needs, and one of the most important is shelter, or a home. As we emerge into adult life we face some important questions: What will I do? What kind of relationships do I want to have? Where will I live?

I look back on my life and wonder how many places I have lived in. If I were to include places I have stayed the night, I could not possibly remember them all.

The few times my wife and I have gone house-hunting have been quite a mixture of excitement, tedium and even despair. On one occasion my wife and I had looked at many different houses. None of them felt like places we would like to settle into. And then we came to the home we ended up buying. We knew at once that this was to be our home. We have now lived in it for over twenty years.

What would it be like to die and wake up in the spiritual world? How could we find where to live? Swedenborg wrote that house-hunting after death is very simple and rewarding. As we wake up from the process we call dying, we are led to a place, already prepared and furnished for us, that we know is our home. We feel as if we have always lived there, because our spiritual homes are manifestations of our own minds. The structures and furnishings are all a reflection of what we love. It is as if the house is an expression of who we are.

Since after death we go through many changes, our houses will also change according to our varying moods and our spiritual growth. Throughout the process, the house will be so much in keeping with our inner nature that we will always feel totally at home there. What a blessing that will be!

"Even though there is space in heaven as there is in our world, nothing there is evaluated on the basis of space, but only on the basis of state."

HEAVEN AND HELL 198

CHAPTER 22

Space in Heaven

A friend of mine had failing health. He had been sick for some time and knew that he was not long for this world. He talked to me about his wife, who had died about twenty years before. He seemed concerned about getting to see her again, so I assured him that when people die and wake up in the spiritual world, they normally meet the people they have known and loved on earth.

My answer did not alleviate his fears. "I know we will meet again," he said, "but will we stay together?"

I answered him by saying that, since space in the spiritual world is determined by state of mind, we will be near the people we love and far apart from people we do not love. Those who are spiritually connected need not fear being wrenched apart. Spiritual closeness is also spatial closeness in the spiritual world.

On earth we can be physically separated from those we care about, but after death we are always with the people we love. Just as they are near to us in heart, so we see them as being near to us in fact. If we think of someone, that person is instantly present as if he or she had been summoned.

It is interesting to see how technology has created something like this condition even on earth. If we think of someone we love, we might be able to speak to that person within seconds, thanks to the global telephone service or online video chats. And if we can't speak, maybe we can communicate by e-mail or text messaging.

One of the most beautiful promises about life after death is that we will always be close to the people we care about and love. Love conquers distance and brings our loved ones near.

"We have been created in the image of heaven and
in the image of this world, our inner being in the image
of heaven and our outer in the image of this world."

HEAVEN AND HELL 202

CHAPTER 23

The Structure of Heaven and the Interconnectedness of Angels

The human brain has been described as the most highly organized substance in the universe. The brain contains more cells than there are people in the world, each cell linked in such a way as to enable it to communicate with other cells. Through the brain stem, these cells are connected to all parts of the body. The heart also connects with different parts of the body through its network of blood vessels. In fact, all our bodily systems are interconnected in an amazing, organized fashion. This marvelous order enables the body, with all of its different parts and organs, to function as a single unit.

Heaven functions in a similar way. The angels are interconnected, which enables an angel to make a contribution to the welfare of the whole of heaven and to benefit from the gifts of all the other angels. In a remarkable way, each angel is like a focal point for all of the love and inspiration of all the other angels. Heaven is amazingly constructed.

We have our own systems in this world, and they become more complex with every passing year. I can remember visiting a telephone exchange office about fifty years ago and being told that every phone in the country could have a direct connection to any other phone in the country through switchboards. The system did not work overseas except through a clumsy and far-from-perfect radio system. Now the telephone system is not only more complex, but we have the whole Internet system enabling a person with a home computer and a telephone connection to send messages over the World Wide Web.

These technological systems enable us to keep in touch with people in this world. On an emotional and spiritual level, our minds and hearts are part of the heavenly communication system made possible by the marvelous structure of heaven. We can be in touch with the whole range of heaven because of the spiritual connections we have with that higher plane of existence. After death we will be much more aware of this wonderful interconnectedness, and we will be able to experience more consciously the benefits of the widespread giving and receiving that angels enjoy.

"In the heavens there is no government except the government of mutual love, and the government of mutual love is heavenly government."

HEAVEN AND HELL 213

CHAPTER 24

Government in Heaven

Imagine a community consisting entirely of people who love each other and who would not dream of hurting each other. They wouldn't think of taking anything that was not theirs. They would be upset to think that they might have caused another person pain. They would respect each other's relationships, and it would be totally unthinkable to them to be unfaithful. Such a community would have no need of prisons or police.

In such a community there might still be differences of opinion and times when people who disagree might seek the counsel of someone wiser or more experienced than themselves. If it came to settling a problem, the intervention would be done lovingly and would look to the best outcome for everyone involved.

Wouldn't a community that operated with such mutual love and respect be heaven? Well, this imagined community is what heaven is like. For the sake of working out disagreements or settling problems, there are a variety of different forms of government in the many communities in heaven. Each form of government is a perfect fit for the people in that community. There are various kinds of officials, depending upon the kind or number of officials a community wants. There are laws that the members of the community have agreed to live by, and the officials manage everything according to those laws, going to God for guidance in their decisions.

Every form of government in heaven shares a central focus on the public good and, within that focus, the good of each individual. With great wisdom and kindness, angels work together to create a life within their communities that is based on mutual love.

Everyone in all heaven is under the guidance of the Lord, who loves everyone and who from his divine love arranges things so that it is the common good from which individuals receive what is good for them. (*Heaven and Hell* 217)

*"Angels are constantly being perfected
in wisdom and love."*

HEAVEN AND HELL 221

CHAPTER 25

Worship in Heaven

For people who know the Lord and adore him in their hearts, every day is a day of worship. They lift up their minds in prayer as they greet each new day. Before they go to sleep, they close the day with a prayer. When facing difficulties they turn to God. When joyful about good news, they are grateful to God. They see all of the different aspects of the day as part of their life of worship. They accept their responsibilities as an expression of devotion to God and to others. In their caring for other people, they show how much they care about God. All of the elements of worship are in their day-to-day interactions with other people—joy, gratitude, humility, a willingness to learn and a desire to serve.

Many angels also enjoy coming together in formal worship services, because they are eager to learn more about becoming wiser and more loving. To them a formal worship service feels like a privilege rather than an obligation and is more like recreation than work. Having an attitude of reverence for every aspect of life, their spirits soar when they hear the message, "Today is the Sabbath." They love to continue to learn from the depths of the Word, and they enjoy doing so with their deeply-loved friends. Preachers who have a special love for teaching give talks that far surpass any sermons that are given on earth.

In a sense, every day in heaven is a day of worship, because worship is the whole of the life of angels. What a difference it makes to our earthly life when we experience this ongoing worship during the week, and how wonderful it is to have a worship service to begin a new week. Thank you, Lord.

"*Angels take absolutely no credit to themselves and turn
down any praise or admiration for anything they have
done, but attribute it all to the Lord.*"

HEAVEN AND HELL 230

CHAPTER 26

The Power of the Angels

Occasionally I hear people expressing concern about the state of the world and the negative forces that seem, at times, to be overwhelming. Fortunately evil does not really have any lasting power. Though it often seems that evil can exert control over good people, this appearance is always temporary. In the long run the only power in the universe is the power of God, which is also the power of good.

The Hebrew word for God is *El*, a word that also means strong, mighty, a mighty one, power. Angels, as messengers of God, are also given power. They have power to the extent that they allow the Lord's power to fill them and to the extent that they recognize the source of that power. With that power, angels can knock down anything in the spiritual world that threatens to block out God's influence, whether it be a mountain or an army. Angels can cause an evil person to faint simply by looking at that person, because an evil person cannot handle the power of God's love that flows through the angels.

Jesus talks about the "power of darkness" (Luke 22:53) but this power cannot last. In the end darkness has no power at all. If you have a box with a partition in the middle, one side of the partition being full of light and the other side full of darkness, what happens when the partition is removed? The light simply fills both sections. The darkness has no power to extinguish the light.

Why then should the Bible talk about "the power of darkness?" Isn't it because people are deceived into ascribing power to the darkness? For example, lies only have power when people believe them to be true! As soon as the truth is revealed in a situation, the lies dissipate. Lies may block out the truth for a while, but they can never destroy it. As soon as the lie is removed, the truth floods in like light filling a previously dark space. The gospel of John says "the light shines in the darkness, and the darkness did not comprehend it." (John 1:5) The lasting power is in the light of truth. From the power of God's truth filling them, angels have tremendous power against the forces of evil that want to create destructive lies.

And what about the power of love? Love is actually the driving force behind all power in the universe. Angels could not have any power from truth unless they were also letting God's love fill them, because God does not want truth to be used in any way that is not loving. The angels have power in great abundance, because they are happy to acknowledge the Lord God as the real source of the love that fills their hearts. It is said that "love conquers all," and this is very true. Love has the power to last forever, to create real bonds, to stop conflicts, to keep someone going despite adversity, and much more. And so when angels tap into the love from God, the source of all real love, they are tapping into the love that can never be destroyed. God's love is a never-ending source of strength and power.

The power of God through angels affects every moment of our lives and is an important factor in our spiritual protection. Angels bring us power from God's love to take all the actions we need to live a life of kindness and integrity.

"There was one particular hard-hearted spirit with whom an angel talked, and eventually he was so moved by what the angel was saying that he burst into tears, saying that he couldn't help it, love was talking, and he had never cried before."

HEAVEN AND HELL 238

CHAPTER 27

Angelic Communication

As I write this I am preparing for a trip to Sweden. I am studying a few Swedish phrases to add to the enjoyment of my trip. It is not my intention to learn to speak Swedish well. I have tried that with French and Dutch, and I never got to the point where I was fluent. Learning another language is extremely difficult, but I find it relatively easy to pick up a few words and phrases. I'm sure that doing so will add a richness to my experience of traveling in Sweden.

How sad it is that we are divided in this earthly life by so many different languages. This barrier is one of the problems that is solved by death. After we die we lose nothing that belongs to us as human beings, but we do lose our earthly languages. They are of no use to us in the spiritual world where there is a different language—one that is learned spontaneously and without effort, one that is universal. This heavenly language is the language of thought. In a sense you could say that we already know this language. All we have to do is think, and our minds are speaking it fluently.

Of course language requires feelings as well. Swedenborg found that the angelic language is a perfect expression of both the feelings and the thoughts of the speakers. Angelic language involves facial expressions, inflections, and tones as well as words. It is full of wisdom since it comes from angels' deepest thoughts, and it is full of love because it always comes from the heart.

There are stories in the Bible of angels speaking to people on earth. There is never a need for an interpreter, since the angel communicates by ideas which are translated in the mind of the listeners into their own languages. The words sound to the earthly listener as if the angel is speaking Hebrew or Swedish or whatever their own language might be. It would be more accurate to say that the angels are sharing ideas which come into the listeners' awareness in the human languages that they know.

*"When angels talk with us they turn toward us
and unite with us."*

HEAVEN AND HELL 246

CHAPTER 28

How Angels Talk with People

Imagine a teenager talking to a parent. The teen has been reading the Bible and noticing that angels sometimes talk with people, like the one who talked with Abraham. Then comes the question: "Could an angel talk to me?"

As a parent who has read Swedenborg's descriptions about heaven and angels, I might engage in a conversation with that teenager that went something like this:

"Could an angel talk to me?"

"Good question. Yes, I believe it is possible for an angel to talk with you. It is not very likely, because most of the time we're paying attention to earthly influences rather than heavenly influences, but it is possible."

"If angels did talk to me, would they have to know my language?"

"They are able to connect with your memory and use your language."

"What would it sound like? Would it be all spooky and mysterious?"

"No, it would sound just like someone was standing near you and talking with you."

"Would people near me be able to hear it?"

"The sound wouldn't be caused by waves traveling through the air and then into your ear. Instead an angel's speech would come in through your thoughts and then move into your ear from within. As far as the sound goes, you would not be able to tell the difference, but people around you wouldn't hear anything."

"Would the angel tell me all kinds of things nobody else knows?"

"Angels are careful not to go beyond what you already know. In talking with you, they connect with your memory so they can use a language and thoughts that are familiar to you. But let me ask you a question. What would you want to talk about?"

"I know lots of people would want to know about the future—yes, and maybe I might want to know something like who I am going to marry."

"But angels are not able to see the future, and even if they were they would be careful not to tell you."

"Why not?"

"Because it would have too much influence on you. It could rob you of the challenge of using your own mind and heart to make your own decision."

"I might want to ask them about the Lord."

"Yes, that would be good. They would probably answer by reminding you to read the Bible to find out for yourself."

"I have heard that there are evil spirits. What would happen if one of those started talking to me?"

"You would have a problem. It's like people who date on the Internet. How do they know whether the people on the other end are genuine or are just messing with their minds? If you found that the spirit was saying cruel and ugly things and kept putting pressure on you, you could be pretty sure it was an evil spirit. There are mental illnesses in which people hear voices telling them cruel or dangerous things. These illnesses are often evil spirits talking."[2]

"Do many people talk with angels?"

"In ancient civilizations some did. Not so many do these days, I guess because so many people are attached to the physical world. Angels are not interested in talking with people who can only think of pleasure and money. The word 'angel' originally meant a messenger, and in the Bible angels speak to people in order to bring messages from God."

"Should I try to make contact with angels?"

"Probably not, unless you really think it is the Lord's will and you want to learn about spiritual things. One day an angel might speak with you, probably saying only a few words and leaving you with a feeling that it might have been a dream. Angels operate this way because they do not at all want to put pressure on you. They trust you to choose for yourself to live a good life."

Angels want nothing else than to serve the Lord and help their fellow human beings. If these things can be accomplished by an angel conversing with one of us, then the angel will do so in a way that is kind and gentle and that preserves our freedom.

"Since angels do have language and their language is
one of words, they also have written materials."

HEAVEN AND HELL 258

CHAPTER 29

Angelic Writing

Anyone who has attempted to write a book knows that it requires a special kind of effort to put ideas in writing, quite different from the process of speaking. By putting something in writing, the author provides a gift for the world. In some cases the books continue to enrich people's lives over hundreds and even thousands of years. For many people books are among life's greatest treasures.

I was once visiting a friend, and I couldn't help noticing the great quantity of books in his home. There were bookcases everywhere, crammed with books on a wide variety of subjects like languages ancient and modern, history, and science. There were dictionaries, encyclopedias and all kinds of reference works. I could have spent weeks just browsing through those fascinating tomes.

Since when we die we take all our genuine interests with us, it follows that our love of reading will still be with us in the next life. Do the angels have bookcases? Are their homes full of reading materials? For any angel that gains delight from books and reading, the answer to these questions is yes.

There are stories in the Bible where a person on earth sees into heaven. The prophet Ezekiel had a vision of heaven, and in that vision he saw an angel with the scroll of a book, written on both sides. (Ezekiel 2:9,10) Ezekiel was commanded to eat the book. He found that it was sweet in his mouth. The same thing happened to John on the Isle of Patmos. He writes about taking a book from an angel, eating it, and finding it sweet in his mouth but bitter in his stomach. (Revelation 10:9,10)

These stories show not only that written materials exist in heaven, but also that they are of a very different nature than ours! Even the written characters themselves are very different from those on earth. Each written letter or accent in heaven contains an amazing amount of wisdom, so the angels are able to gain and learn much from just a few written characters.

The main reason for writing in heaven is so that the "Word of God" can exist there in the form of the Bible. When angels read the Bible do they see the same stories that we see when we read it? Yes, but from a totally different point of view—not as earthly stories, but as stories about the infinite love and wisdom of God.

When angels write, they do so to express things that they are thinking about and feeling, very much like we do here on earth. However the writing of angels flows quickly and spontaneously from their thoughts. There is no hovering over the page, trying to decide on just the right word. The words and characters available to them perfectly reflect what they are trying to say and communicate. And of course the things that they want to communicate are always filled with heavenly love and wisdom.

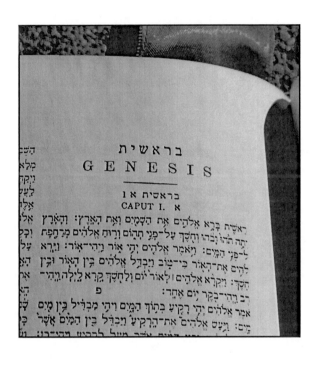

"Heaven is where everyone shares everything of value."
HEAVEN AND HELL 268

CHAPTER 30

Angelic Wisdom

One of the great tasks in life is to seek for wisdom. The process begins early in life and continues forever!

I can remember being in situations where older and wiser people than myself were having a discussion. They were tossing ideas back and forth like beanbags. I was impressed by these people. In addition I seemed to myself to become wiser just by participating in the discussion. It was as if the brilliance of the speakers illuminated me and made me a little smarter than I was.

In the spiritual world, wisdom manifests itself as light. When we think of the light of heaven shining so much brighter than light in this world, we can get some idea of the wisdom of the angels. And though we can get glimpses now and then of the light that angels live in, that light is mostly inaccessible to us on earth.

There are five main ingredients that make up the wisdom of angels:

1. Because of their integrity, the higher levels of their minds are open and transparent. The angels do not put any effort into trying to deceive or trying to impress one another.
2. They have so much light because it shines out from the warmth of their love. Just as heat brings light in this world, it is the love of the angels in heaven that makes them wise. True wisdom has everything to do with using knowledge for kind and loving purposes.
3. They are without ego. They love truth because it is true, and not for the sake of any credit to themselves or personal gain.
4. They openly and gladly share their wisdom with others. When an angel joins a group of other angels, he or she immediately shares the ideas and perceptions of all the others. In this case the whole is greater than the sum of its parts. Through this sharing, each angel becomes wiser.
5. The angels long for truth the way a starving person hungers for food. Because of this hunger they continue growing in wisdom forever.

God has a never-ending supply of amazing truth and knowledge to offer us. Because angels want this truth and knowledge not for selfish purposes but for loving and useful purposes, their capacity to receive it makes them brilliantly wise.

*"All the people who are in heaven are in innocence, since
all the people who are there love to be led by the Lord."*

HEAVEN AND HELL 280

CHAPTER 31

Angelic Innocence

There is a wonderful scene in the movie *Star Wars* when Luke first meets Yoda. Luke is looking for a powerful and wise being, and he thinks at first that Yoda is just a child. Luke finds that Yoda is incredibly ancient, wise and strong. There is a similar encounter in the movie *E.T.* when an alien being appears to be very young and ineffective, but that appearance proves to be untrue. Both can be used to illustrate a profound truth about the angels of heaven, namely that they are completely innocent and exceptionally wise.

With little children, innocence comes from the fact that they know very little and have so little power. This ignorance and powerlessness makes them dependent on their parents or other adults. As they grow children become more independent and less innocent.

Jesus said that we have to return to something like the innocence of little children to enter the kingdom of heaven. (Mark 10:14,15) As people age they seem to return to this quality of childhood but with the added element of wisdom.

So what is the innocence of heaven like? Swedenborg defines innocence not as "guiltlessness" or "ignorance" but rather as a "willingness to be led." The innocence of children includes the fact that they are willing to be led and guided by their parents, trusting that their parents will care for them. Angels freely choose to be led and guided by the Lord, and they choose to trust that the Lord is taking care of them. This willingness is the innocence of heaven.

Angelic innocence is what is behind many of the characteristics of angels. They do not have an exaggerated idea of their own importance but attribute what is good to the Lord. They know how dangerous it is to be led by self-will, and they prefer to be led by God. Angels love goodness and delight in the truth. They are content with their lot and are not the least bit worried about the future. They do not act deceitfully with others or try to use cunning to get their own way. When angels hear something true they immediately apply it to their lives. They know that their knowledge, vast as it is compared to our own, is nothing. The little that they know is like a drop of water compared to the whole ocean.

This innocence is the essence of the goodness of heaven. Innocence allows angels to release attitudes that block out God's influence, and innocence leaves angels open to God's loving guidance.

"Peace in the heavens is the divine nature intimately
affecting everything good there with blessedness. So it
is the source of all the joy of heaven."

HEAVEN AND HELL 286

CHAPTER 32

Peace in Heaven

I was once visiting an older woman who lived alone in the remote mountains of Wales. She had something about her that was truly amazing—a kind of contentment. This contentment did not seem to come from her circumstances. She had her share of challenges. Rather her sense of satisfaction with life seemed to come from deep inside. This inner quality brought a glow to everything in her life. I had a strong feeling that she had found the secret of happiness. She was at peace.

Some look for peace to come from external sources, as if it could come from the absence of strife or from overcoming problems. But peace is the love of God touching us on the deepest level of our beings, which means that peace essentially is a divine quality. The Creator of the universe is at peace, and those who connect with the Creator, through love, experience that peace. Although I cannot judge, it seems that a peaceful connection with God is what I sensed as present with the woman in Wales.

Innocence and peace are the deepest aspects of heaven. Innocence is the source of all the goodness of heaven, and peace is a source of all the joy.

People who return from a near-death experience sometimes describe having had a most peaceful and delightful time, so much so that they were extremely reluctant to return to their usual state of life in this world. Some manage to hold onto that inner peace when they do return, and it changes the whole quality of their lives.

So long as we live on this natural plane, it is inevitable that we are tossed about in various ways, and we long for peace. The nearest we might get is contentment in God. To work toward achieving greater peace, we can work on our connection with the Prince of Peace. When we feel the joy of God in our hearts, we are experiencing something of that peace of heaven, peace that passes all understanding, peace that is the ultimate goal of all human striving.

"If we believed the way things really are, that everything good comes from God and everything evil from hell, then we would not take credit for the good within us or blame for the evil."

HEAVEN AND HELL 302

CHAPTER 33

The Connection Between Heaven and Earth

A person was hiking alone in the mountains and stopped to rest. For a moment she felt quite alone and began thinking how small she was in a remote area of this tiny planet with its medium-sized sun and average galaxy, all in an unimaginably-large universe. But the feeling soon passed as she stopped to think of her connections with that other world—the more real world of the spirit. She knew that God was directly present with her as her very life. She also knew that the angels of God were always present—not seen, but sensed in a feeling of peace and contentment.

Then she began to have doubts and fears. Her mind was chilled by anxieties that robbed her of her peace. At first she was alarmed by this. The anxieties seemed to wipe away all the good feelings of her previous state of mind. But then she remembered that, just as we have angels and good spirits around us who always wish us well, we also have evil spirits with us who want to bring us trouble. We do not see them, but we can tell that they are present by the anxiety we feel and the dark and negative thinking they bring. Remembering this concept was very helpful for this woman. She found that she could tell those evil spirits to get behind her as she raised her mind to heavenly thoughts and feelings.

Yes, we live in a physical world, but we are also very connected with the spiritual world. In fact, since we are living beings because of our spirits rather than our bodies, we couldn't live at all without this connection. Angels are present with us at all times, and the Lord God never leaves us. The Lord flows directly into the deepest parts of us. But, since it takes many years of growth and learning to become more in accord with the pattern of heaven, we also have spirits near us who are not yet angels and who act as intermediaries. These companions are spirits who are still developing before they can enter heaven and are therefore more like us.

Also, in order that we can have free choice, we have evil spirits near us. These good and evil spirits are living their own lives, but they are near us because the things they love are similar to the things that we love. Since these spirits are close to us, we will feel feelings that arise from either the good or the evil spirits. Then we have a choice as to which feelings we will accept and adopt as our own.

After some time of vacillation between positive and negative feelings, the woman hiking in the mountains remembered another important principle. The Lord and heaven also communicate with us through the Bible. So she took out her Bible and began to read:

> God is our refuge and strength, a very present help in trouble. Therefore we will not fear, though the earth be removed, and though the mountains be carried into the midst of the sea. (Psalm 46:1,2)

This reading brought an immediate change of mood. She felt connected to heaven again.

We are connected with the spiritual world at all times. Accepting and adopting good and positive feelings instead of harmful and negative feelings connects us with heaven. Also we can strengthen that connection by reading the Bible. Though Bible stories may seem to be concerned about events in the world, the deeper meanings of the stories are about heavenly matters and thus connect us with heaven itself.

"When we read the Word and grasp it in its
literal or outward meaning, angels grasp it
in its inner or spiritual meaning."

HEAVEN AND HELL 306

CHAPTER 34

Heaven's Connection With Us Through the Bible

There are many different ways to celebrate Christmas. My father usually worked on Christmas Eve and bought a tree from the sellers in Philadelphia before taking the train home. The younger children were in bed before the tree was put up and decorated. One year my father was either short of money or shopped too late, and the tree he brought home was rather pathetic. We sang to it, "O cheesy tree." But the fact that the tree wasn't perfect didn't matter, since the big event on Christmas morning was not so much about the tree, which we saw as we came downstairs singing "Come, all ye faithful." The big event was having the family gather around as Dad read the Christmas story from the Bible. He could not get through the reading without a tear or two.

Picture our room full of people: grandparents in their eighties, parents, aunts and uncles in their fifties or sixties, and children ranging from teens down to infants. We were each very different in our personalities and in our stages of life. We each took something different from the reading. And we were bonded together by hearing a reading of the Gospel.

This picture comes to mind as I think of the teaching in *Heaven and Hell* that people on earth and angels in heaven are connected through the Word of God. A person on earth might be reading the creation story in Genesis, thinking about light and darkness, sky, sea and land, plants and animals, all arriving in their own time. An angel hearing this story would not be thinking about physical and earthly things at all. He or she would be thinking about the deeper message in the story, about how people emerge from the darkness of ignorance and falsity into the light of true understanding. The Word of God has a special power to connect heaven and earth.

I attended a workshop for people interested in church growth. The closing worship was performed in a circle of about a dozen people. Instead of having one of the ministers present read a passage or two from the Bible, we were all invited to think of some Bible verse, take it out of our memories and speak it aloud. One by one, voices came from the circle: "Be not afraid,"

"In my Father's house are many mansions," "If you love me, keep my commandments" and so on and on. Every person in the circle had a number of different Bible verses that meant a great deal to him or her. The effect of having verses spoken aloud by men and women, ordained and lay, young and old, was very touching. We had a profound sense that angels attended us in that little circle and that, through those passages, heaven and earth were one.

When we read the Bible, we affect the angels who are connected with us, and they think about the deeper meanings of the stories. Then, especially if we have some sense that the stories have a deeper meaning, the feelings and the insights of those angels will affect us as well.

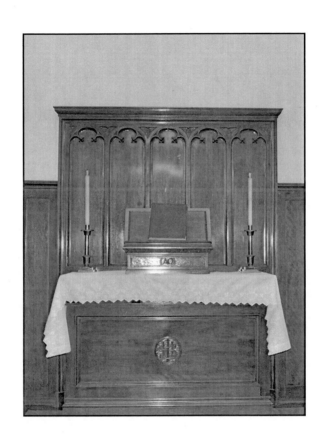

"All the people in heaven and in hell are from the human race—in heaven the ones who have lived in heavenly love and faith, and in hell the ones who have lived in hellish love and faith."

HEAVEN AND HELL 311

CHAPTER 35

Heaven and Hell Are From the Human Race

What are angels, and where do they come from? For years there has been a belief that, before God created the world, he created angels and that human beings are a totally separate race. In contrast to that, we often hear people talk about a loved one in terms that suggest that, having died, the loved one is now an angel.

So who are angels? Swedenborg's long experiences of the spiritual realm taught him a very simple principle: all angels began life as people born into this physical existence that we live in. Angels are not a separate creation by God but are instead people just like the ones we know on earth. Television shows like "Touched by an Angel" support this idea. The angels in that show look so much like ordinary people that, through most of each episode, they are thought to be earthly humans. The general impression that good people become angels after death is one that many people seem to have a natural affinity for. According to Swedenborg, each one of us is intended to become an angel after we die.

Many people believe this idea instinctively. Many also have a strong sense that people they know in this world have angelic qualities: people often say something like "you are such an angel." Once again the general impression comes from an instinctive feeling for the truth.

This earthly life is the training ground for us to begin to learn what angelic life is like. There are two main qualifications for eventually becoming an angel in heaven: a love of God and a love of other people. Whenever we act lovingly and speak wisely, we are all angels-in-training, messengers of God.

*"The Lord's church is spread through the whole world.
It is universal, then, and consists of all individuals who
have lived in the virtue of thoughtfulness according to
the principles of their religions."*

HEAVEN AND HELL 328

CHAPTER 36

The Gentiles

There are many words used by Christians to describe non-Christians. Most of them have come to have a strongly negative connotation. Looking up the root meanings in my old copy of *The Concise Etymological Dictionary of the English Language*, I found some possible reasons for this negativity. Here, in my own words, is how I understood the root meanings.

ALIEN: Someone other than us.
BARBARIAN: A stammerer; someone whose language sounds to us like babble.
FOREIGN: Out-of-doors; someone not within our little world.
GENTILE: Belonging to some other clan or tribe.
HEATHEN: Wild.
INFIDEL: A person without faith.
PAGAN: A villager or person who lives in the country—people who were often thought of as the slowest to accept new ideas.
PRIMITIVE: The first people; the earliest ones.
SAVAGE: Belonging to the forest.
STRANGER: Someone on the outside.

I guess we are all a little wary of "strangers," but in the Christian world this fear has turned into the doctrine that only Christians can be saved. Many of us have had the experience of meeting someone from a totally different culture and religious background, only to find them in some ways more spiritual than the Christians we have known!

Isn't it strange that not only do many Christians deny the possibility of heaven to "pagans," but they even deny it to other branches of Christianity. Sadly, this attitude can even extend to members of their own faith community. Such Christians seem to take the stance of an old adage adapted to say: "No one is really Christian but me and thee . . . and sometimes I wonder about thee!"

The reality is that the mercy of the Lord is far greater than our own. In the Lord's sight everyone on the planet has been born for heaven. Even though there are many false concepts in the seemingly endless forms that religion takes, to get into heaven you need only two true concepts:

1. A belief in God—or at least a belief in something higher than yourself, and
2. A desire to live a good life according to what you believe to be true.

If we have this basis, then any additional true concepts can be taught to us by angels after death. In this way, people of all religions will enter the spiritual world after death on an equal footing, and well-intentioned people from any faith background will enter heaven.

"No one is born for hell—everyone is born for heaven."
HEAVEN AND HELL 329

CHAPTER 37

Little Children in Heaven

One of the saddest of all human experiences is the death of little children. We cannot believe that a merciful God would let one of these little ones perish. But if we could see the other side of their transition, we would at least see that we needn't worry about them. Though the loss is wrenching on the earthly side, we would see that these children are cared for in the spiritual world with amazing tenderness.

If we could watch the unfolding of the new lives of children who have passed over, we would notice angels lovingly watching over them and angel parents welcoming them. We would see the children's bright, innocent eyes, full of wonder as they begin exploring their new world. We would enjoy watching them learning, in a spontaneous and imaginative way, all of the things they would need to know. We would see them dancing through the meadows with garlands of flowers and beauty all around. We would see their new families adopt them into angelic foster homes, with perfect care to their every need.

It would be exciting to watch them learn to walk, speak and read without effort. It would be thrilling to see the eagerness with which they would drink in the teachings of the Bible. We would enjoy being with them as they were taught by pageants and plays, each one designed to communicate some important truth and some deep feeling.

We would watch them grow "physically" as they grew in wisdom and love, their growing bodies perfectly reflecting their spiritual growth. We would eventually see them attain young womanhood and young manhood, the age that they would stay forever.

We might even see them pairing off, finding themselves led by the Lord to a perfect married partner with whom they would then live to eternity.

Would we see the tantrums and selfishness that children on earth experience? Yes, to some extent we would, because it is important for them to know the difference between their hereditary instincts and their spiritual life. But among their angel caretakers and teachers, children in the spiritual world have excellent guidance to recognize and put aside any negative tendencies, and to instead open up to the Lord's guidance.

And what of non-Christian children? Would they be there? Yes indeed. A merciful God would not exclude a child from heaven simply because the parents were not Christians. God does not require the external ceremony of baptism as a gateway to heaven, but rather the spiritual process which baptism represents.

In short, if we saw these children, we would still feel sad at our own loss, but we could rest assured that their lives are not over and that their lives were not wasted. Heaven is a place brimming with love for children, and they are raised and cared for in that environment. When we ourselves someday enter the spiritual world, a beloved child who had seemed to leave us too soon will be right there to greet us.

*"To be loved by the Lord is to love the Lord as well,
because love is reciprocal."*

HEAVEN AND HELL 350

CHAPTER 38

Wisdom in Heaven

In this world of IQ testing, SAT scores and numerous other measurements of intelligence, most of us can't help feeling rather dull. I have been in situations where the conversation was so far above my head that I was struggling for air. Not normally shy, I have found that in those situations I don't dare to open my mouth for fear of sounding stupid.

Reading about the wisdom of angels, the question that naturally arises is whether we are likely to feel similarly shy or stupid in heaven. Could we really "fit in" there? Though Swedenborg writes that we will all become angels when we enter heaven, we might wonder if we could ever achieve the wisdom that we imagine angels to have.

And then I remember times when I have been talking with a farmer, leaning over the back fence, feeling totally comfortable, not feeling stupid at all, and at the same time having a wonderful sense that I am in the presence of real wisdom. I have had the same experience talking with a grandmother whose education did not reach past high school, but whose words were very profound.

A worry about being able to "fit in" with wise angels comes from a mistaken definition of "wise." In this world, the word "wise" is often used in connection with people who are particularly scholarly or learned. So what about just plain simple folk? Can they fit in with those wise angels?

What is it that produces wisdom? It is certainly not intelligence. There are very intelligent people who are not wise at all. Wisdom does not come from education. There are people who have had little formal education and have achieved great wisdom, and there are many highly-educated people who lack common sense. Wisdom comes from a love of truth, not for glory, but just because it is true. The truth that a person loves doesn't have to be sophisticated or impressive to others. There is a lot of truth in life that is very down-to-earth and simple. People who love the truth that they find as they work their way through life are on the path to wisdom.

Some people who delight in truth become seekers. They are

not content with sham and are deeply affected by and delighted with truth when they find it. Such people aren't interested in just accumulating knowledge. What they learn they translate directly into their lives. They do not understand what it is to learn just for the sake of learning. To them truth is a tool for learning to love and for learning to live a good life. Such people, seeking truth for these purposes, show us the nature of the wisdom of angels.

We can increase our capacity for wisdom by getting in touch with our own love of truth and by looking especially for those ideas that will make us better citizens of this world and the next. In this way we can approach the wisdom of the angels.

"No one is shut out of heaven for having abundant possessions or accepted into heaven because of poverty."
HEAVEN AND HELL 357

CHAPTER 39

The Rich and the Poor in Heaven

Is having material wealth good or bad for our spiritual life? Jesus said: "It is hard for a rich person to enter the kingdom of heaven." (Matthew 19:23) Some Christians have deliberately made themselves poor because of this saying. But most of us live with the idea that material wealth is a good thing (why else would there be such a fervor over lotteries?). The fact is that Jesus was talking about being poor "in spirit." (Matthew 5:3) He was talking about humility.

Are worldly riches curses or blessings? There is a very simple answer: if you are striving to live a good life and to serve your fellow human beings, whatever amount of wealth you have is all right.

> Heaven is for everyone who lives a life of faith and love, whether rich or poor. . . . I have been granted sure knowledge that rich people enter heaven just as easily as poor people do, and that no one is shut out of heaven for having abundant possessions or accepted into heaven because of poverty. (*Heaven and Hell* 357)

We have been born into this world and we need to come to terms with it. Seeking to be financially successful is perfectly all right, so long as the success is not achieved by fraud or deceit, and so long as the motivations are not greedy or materialistic. We are allowed to enjoy the good things of life, provided we do not make them more important than spiritual things.

As far as our judgments of others are concerned, we need to be careful not to make judgments about people's spiritual state on the basis of the amount of money they have, whether it is great or small. Money itself is totally neutral. Our handling of money can be good or evil.

Our spiritual states are more important than our bank accounts, and our degrees of usefulness to others are more important than our salaries. We need to keep our lives in the proper balance.

"Marriage in the heavens
is the union of two people into one mind."
HEAVEN AND HELL 367

CHAPTER 40

Marriages in Heaven

I love helping couples prepare for their weddings. For many of them it is the most significant event of their entire life. I talk with the couples about various aspects of marriage, especially the fact that it is a partnership of people who are equal and different.

Naturally we think of love as being the most important ingredient in marriage, but I like to point out that love is not a feeling. Love lies deeper than our feelings and gives rise to them. Love is a kind of inner consent that says "YES" to this other person and says "YES" to working with that person to create a life-long bond of friendship, cooperation, respect and affection. Love is a commitment and a decision.

Many couples agree that falling in love was a spiritual event for them. I offer all couples a selection of readings that can be used for their wedding service, including some from Swedenborg's works that talk about the eternity of marriage. The couples come from a variety of religious backgrounds, and I have noticed that most of them choose passages about marriage after death, even some couples whose religious tradition does not include that idea. Love seems to create its own perception and its own wisdom. The feeling of love is "this is forever."

There is a song from the musical *West Side Story* that some couples choose to have sung at their wedding. The song is called "One Hand, One Heart" and it includes the lyrics: "Only death will part us now." Just as I am beginning to feel uncomfortable about these words the message shifts, and the last verse says: "Even death won't part us now."[3]

According to Swedenborg, there is marriage after death. Jesus seemed to say that there is no marriage in heaven (Matthew 22:30), but that was because his listeners thought of marriage as little more than the ownership of a wife as property. They would not have been able to fathom the kind of marriage that exists in heaven.

Heavenly marriage exists between one man and one woman, and those two can be people who had been married to each other on earth if they truly loved each other on a spiritual level. The force that binds them together is the force of the divine love joining them into a oneness that is full of tenderness and delight.

I do believe that people who marry for love marry in the hope that their love will last, not just for a few years on earth, but forever. If an eternal marriage is what they truly want, and if they work on making their love last and grow, then this wish will come true.

"The Lord's kingdom is a kingdom of uses."
HEAVEN AND HELL 387

CHAPTER 41

The Jobs of Angels

Which would you rather have: eternal idleness or ongoing useful activity? Swedenborg found that, in heaven, much joy comes from the satisfaction of doing something useful. He noted that, just as every organ and cell in the body has to make a contribution to the welfare of the whole system, so every angel and every community of angels is involved in usefulness to others. Indeed this usefulness is a real source of heavenly joy and happiness!

The angels have jobs, and they love their work. They have times of rest and recreation, too, but rest and recreation would feel empty if angels did not also have enjoyable tasks to keep them feeling challenged and interested in life.

But what jobs do the angels have? We know that there are guardian angels. There are angels who are with people as they die, and other angels who help these people as they wake up in the spiritual world. Some angels have the work of welcoming people who die in infancy and raising them in heaven. Other angels are sent to protect people on earth from harm.

But the majority of the jobs of the angels would be a total mystery to us. They have a thousand times as many occupations available to them as we do on earth, and most of these occupations are beyond our present understanding.

To get some idea of this gap in understanding, imagine visiting a hunter-gatherer community. The community is self-contained, and the needs of everyone are provided for, but the jobs are very limited. Some community members are employed in making tools, others in finding game, still others in preparing food, building shelters, possibly making utensils, clothing and fabrics, and so on. It would not take you long to list all the jobs available in such a community. You would also find that each individual might have several different things to do to help the group survive. Could you explain to them the various jobs in our modern cities? How many of those jobs do you understand yourself?

Project your imagination into the future of life on this planet. If you could be transported to the year AD 3000 and look at the jobs people would be doing, how many of their jobs could you understand?

One more leap of imagination takes you to the spiritual world, to heaven and the occupations of the angels. Angelic occupations are far more numerous than jobs on earth, far more satisfying (because each person does what he or she loves to do), and far more valuable. The kingdom of heaven is a kingdom of useful activities, and it is through these activities that the angels find their deepest satisfaction.

"For everyone [in heaven], it is delightful to share
their pleasure and bliss with someone else."

HEAVEN AND HELL 399

CHAPTER 42

Angelic Happiness

A man was searching for the truth. On hearing that there was a wise guru sitting on a mountain, the man made the arduous journey up the mountain so that he could pose a burning question: "What is the purpose of life?"

Without a moment's hesitation, the guru said: "To be happy."

The man looked very puzzled and a little disappointed at the answer. "Does this mean that I can do whatever I like?"

The guru replied, "The purpose of life is to have the deepest satisfaction and the greatest happiness. You probably have no idea how to be really happy. Try to find happiness. If you need to learn more, you can always come back and ask again."

The man descended the mountain feeling relieved. He did think that his own happiness was the most important thing in the world. He got a job but only went to work when it made him feel good. He got into a relationship but thought only about his own happiness, taking no interest in the happiness of the other person.

After years of self-indulgence and deep disappointment, he decided that he needed to talk to the guru again. So he made the journey back up the mountain.

"What is the purpose of life?" he asked again, as if he had never asked the question before.

"To be happy," said the guru. "I told you that years ago."

"But it doesn't work. I tried it. I lost my job and my friends, and I didn't have that much fun."

"I told you that you did not know how to be happy. How do you feel about your life so far?"

"It has been miserable."

"Do you feel that misery is the purpose of life?"

"No, something is wrong."

"Then you need to learn how to be happy. I will give you a few clues. You will never be truly happy if you live only for yourself or simply indulge your cravings. To be happy you have to find out some way of giving happiness to others and being in meaningful and loving relationships with others. When you learn that, you will know what heaven is, because you will feel heavenly joy. Whether you say heaven or heavenly joy, it amounts to the same thing. What would heaven be like if it were not joyful?"

"Why does it have to be so complicated?"

"It is not really complicated at all, but, for some reason, many people have great difficulty finding real happiness. Please do not settle for some passing pleasure. Eternal happiness is so much better than that."

The man went down the mountain, continued his life and applied the guru's advice. Eventually the man died, and in heaven he happened to meet the guru.

"Well," said the guru, "what do you think now?"

"I have never known such bliss. This happiness far surpasses any idea of joy I had before, and all the struggles to achieve it were completely worthwhile. This happiness really *is* the purpose of life!"

Angelic happiness is an inner and spiritual pleasure. All the pleasures that angels feel flow from their feelings of love for the Lord and for their fellow human beings. The more an angel accepts those loves, the more deeply his or her inner levels become open to the Lord's love. Since the Lord's divine love wants nothing more than the happiness of all people, this love brings with it tremendous happiness. And the more an angel acts to share that happiness with others, the more of that love and bliss can flow in.

*"The uninhabited heaven is so vast
that it could never be filled to all eternity."*

HEAVEN AND HELL 419

CHAPTER 43

The Immensity of Heaven

A parent was having a deep conversation with a ten-year-old child.

"I want to die," said the child.

"Why? Are you feeling depressed?"

"No, I'm feeling great, but I think I'd better die before it is too late."

"Too late for what?"

"You might think this is stupid, but I want to die before heaven gets filled up."

"That would be sad if heaven got filled up, but what makes you think it will?"

"We learned in school that the world population is growing, and even now millions of people die every year. They talk about the world getting overpopulated; well, what about heaven?"

"The fear about overpopulation is because the earth has limited resources. People don't take up much room in this world. In fact you could put the whole population of the world in the Tucson Valley in Arizona. Since angels don't need physical food and don't use up natural resources, there isn't the same problem in heaven as on earth. And in the spiritual world, there is no fixed amount of space as there is in this world. The appearance of space expands according to what is needed—according to how many people are there. The Lord's heart is large enough to love everyone, from all places in the universe, over all time, so heaven will never be full. So please don't be in a hurry to get to heaven. There is no rush. And there is plenty for you to do in this world before you go on to the next one. You are so precious in this world that you should stay here as long as you can, leaving it to the Lord to decide when to call you to heaven."

Heaven is a real place but a spiritual place without physical limitations. It is a place to be close to God, and since God has an infinite desire to draw us all close to him, heaven will always reflect that divine desire and will be ready to welcome more angels. There will always be room for everyone who wants to come to heaven.

The World of Spirits

*"The world of spirits is neither heaven nor hell
but a place or state between the two."*

HEAVEN AND HELL 421

CHAPTER 44

Between Heaven and Hell

Uncle Fred died. The family was gathered for the resurrection service, and people were saying how wonderful it was that Uncle Fred was now an angel in heaven. Some people looked a little bit askance. They knew too much about Uncle Fred to think that all he had to do was to die and go to heaven. It was not that he was such a bad man either. Like most of us he was a mixture—a little of this and a little of that. You couldn't really call him an angel, and you wouldn't think of calling him a devil. He was between heaven and hell.

Very few people are totally ready for heaven or hell when they die. Swedenborg discovered that there is an in-between place in the spiritual world that he called "the world of spirits." On earth, those of us who have lived to adulthood have chosen a general direction either toward heaven or toward hell—either toward a life that serves a greater good or toward a life that is selfish. However, these two general directions are often clouded in this life by a lot of misinformation or painful experiences.

In the "world of spirits," a person has a chance to continue his or her spiritual journey with more clarity and guidance. Misinformation will be corrected. Painful experiences will be fully processed. Bad habits will be released and set aside. Hurtful actions will be clearly seen, so we can stop doing them. We will each have whatever help we desire to do the necessary work that gets us ready for heaven—or, for those who want it, ready for hell. We will all have some work left to do. For those who knew Uncle Fred, it is reassuring to think that he has time to continue his spiritual journey after death and that we will all have time to go through whatever processes we need to experience in order to focus on a heavenly way of life.

In many ways our lives in this world are between heaven and hell. We have our good moments. We know the joy of really caring for other people, and we have times of genuine peace. We have also known the frustration of dealing with our own cravings, our weaknesses and our selfishness. We have already begun the process of choosing our spiritual values and choosing our direction. The more work we do on this process as we live our lives on earth, the readier we will be for the heaven the Lord has provided for us after death.

"It is not the body that thinks, because the body is material. Rather, it is the soul, because the soul is spiritual."

HEAVEN AND HELL 432

CHAPTER 45

Every Person Is a Spirit

Two people were taking a stroll through a beautiful city park. They were very intent on their conversation. They walked alongside the lake, under the great trees, over the bridges and by the fields, talking as they went. After a long while one of them noticed that the sun was setting. They stopped, looked at each other and wondered where they were. They had no sense of how far they had walked or how long. Their bodies had been moving through physical space and time while their minds and hearts were on their own journey—a journey so interesting that it blocked out an awareness of the physical journey.

This type of experience is a reminder that we are spiritual beings. We have a physical life, and to some extent we live in a world of space and time, but the real world we inhabit consists of feelings and thoughts. Our minds (or spirits) even have their own sense of time that is different than physical time, and therefore we can feel that an hour passes as quickly as a minute and minutes can drag on like hours.

Those two people walking in the park were communicating on a spiritual level, and their bodies were like machines going through their normal activities. If through some sudden accident those two people were to be killed simultaneously, they would probably continue walking and talking, scarcely aware that anything had happened! A physical accident cannot harm the spirit or stop what the spirit had been engaged in.

Our internal world is really a spiritual world. It is not material, nor does it have any weight or any time-space dimension. We are not physical beings with a spiritual life. We are spiritual beings with a physical life, which is good news! Our real life, the life that we truly call our own, does not depend on time and space, and so can survive death.

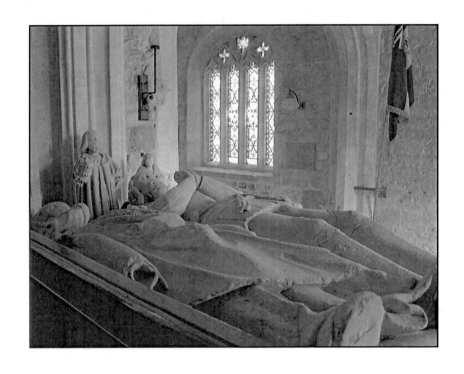

*"When we die we simply move
from one world into another."*

HEAVEN AND HELL 445

CHAPTER 46

What It Is Like To Die

A woman was talking about her own death and about her fears. "I'm not afraid of being dead. I know that we must all die, and I know that God has a place for me in heaven."

"Well, what are you afraid of?" came the response.

"I'm afraid of the process of dying. I see these people who lose their memory, can't walk anymore, have great pain—the process seems to be horrible. That is what I am afraid of."

About twenty years later the woman died. She was almost ninety years old and still living alone without assistance. Her mind was alert, and she had no significant pain. She stood up one day to go and take a nap, an aneurism burst, and within minutes she was gone. What was it like for her to die? It seemed as if it was a pleasant process!

Even for those who have difficult times before their deaths, evidence gathered by Dr. Raymond Moody and others about near-death experiences indicates that the actual time of death involves no pain, fear or stress. Many people who have had near-death experiences report going through a time of great peace and inner calm, even if their bodies had been writhing in agony. The love and beauty that surround them in this near-death experience are so great that they hesitate to return to this world. Evidently dying is very enjoyable.

Amazingly, for the sake of being able to tell us about it, Swedenborg was permitted to go through the process as if he was dying, so that he could describe it in some detail. He found that once the movements of his heart and lungs had completely stopped, his spirit was gently withdrawn from his body and seemed to be lifted up. He noticed that there were angels present with him, sitting silently and holding his mind in thoughts of eternal life. At this time he was soothed by a most beautiful fragrance.

After a while these first angels withdrew and different angels were present, who eventually gave him the use of sight by rolling something like a veil from his eyes. At first the light was a dim blue color. When the light increased to the point where he could see again, he noticed these angels, and they told him that he was a spirit—a person living in the spiritual world. When he returned to earthly consciousness, he wrote about this experience in his journal.

I have read many near-death experience stories that contain similar elements: a feeling of being drawn out of the body and lifted up; a sense of being taken care of; a meeting with angels or spirits who inform the person about what is happening to him or her.

I believe that none of us need to worry about the process of death. God makes sure that the transition between the two worlds is peaceful and safe.

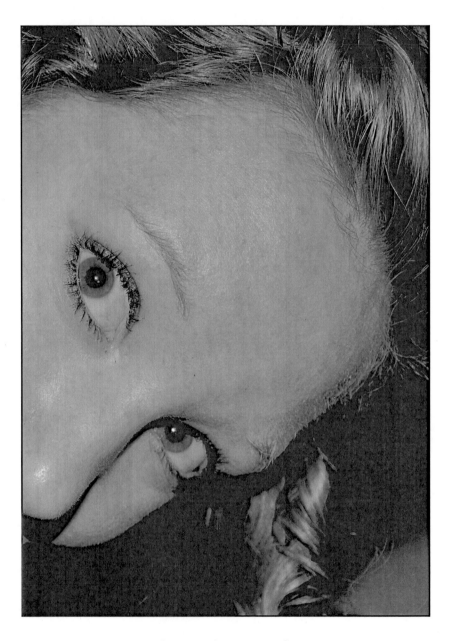

"We are human because of our spirit,
not because of our body."

HEAVEN AND HELL 453

CHAPTER 47

After Death Each Person Is In a Complete Human Form

When we look at another human being, do we just see a physical object? Are we not seeing an expression of feelings and thoughts, purpose and meaning? Are we not seeing something spiritual? We are indeed, because our physical bodies do the bidding of our spirits. In fact our physical bodies are in this human form only because our spirits, or spiritual bodies, are in human form. After death, when we shed our physical bodies, we will fully see and feel our spiritual bodies. Spiritual human bodies are manifestations of what we love and what we think.

In this life, we can sometimes get a glimpse of a person's spirit by looking into his or her eyes. The eyes communicate so many things that are well beyond the merely physical level. We see feelings, determination and intelligence, and these are all spiritual qualities. The whole face is an index of the mind, each part communicating something about the person. A face provides even more information in the spiritual world where we no longer hide what we are thinking or feeling, and it all shows in our faces.

Our spiritual bodies enjoy the five senses, and those senses will be heightened when we live in heaven. The five senses of our physical bodies reflect and symbolize those heavenly senses, even though they are duller in this world. Since eyes and sight in the spiritual world correspond to or symbolize an ability to understand, even in this life we say "I see" when we understand something. In fact many parts of the human body have become symbols for parts of the spirit, because, in the spiritual world, those body parts truly are manifestations of spiritual things. It's no accident that we have expressions like having a "warm heart," being "clear-sighted," being "deaf to what others say," not having much "backbone," not being able to "stomach" something, being "thick-skinned," being able to "stand on our own two feet," and so on.

Swedenborg observed that spiritual bodies look physical, but they are spiritual and obey spiritual laws. The body we seem to have in dreams is something like this. But the spiritual body we have after death is much more real than anything we experience in dreams. Its reality comes from the fact that it expresses who we really are. We need not worry that after death we will be like wisps of smoke or insubstantial beings. We will have bodies that feel solid and real. Unlike the physical body, the spiritual body grows stronger, more vibrant and younger over time, and it never dies.

"When we move from the natural world into the
spiritual . . . we take with us everything that pertains to
our character except our earthly body."

HEAVEN AND HELL 461

CHAPTER 48

The Memory After Death

A woman was telling her friend about her life, and the friend, deeply moved by the story, said: "You ought to write a book."

In a way the woman *was* writing a book—it is called the Book of Life, and it is inscribed on the pages of our memory. We all have such a book. And it is written in indelible ink!

There are times, of course, when we would like to erase a page or two, but, in computer terms, this is a read-only file. If we could change our memory, we would be in danger of losing the good memories along with the bad. But what about the bad memories? Often they involve events that have been some of our greatest teachers. I have heard people describe horrendous chapters in their books of life and then say, "and I wouldn't change it." Why not? Because that chapter was part of their story and contributed to their life in a significant way.

As we age, our memory can become less reliable. This decrease might indicate that after death we would have no memory at all, but the fact is that, although we lose our material possessions and our physical bodies when we die, we do not lose our memories. They have become a part of who we are and thus part of our spirits.

Does this mean that we will forever know our telephone number, social security number, address and a thousand details that have no use after death? In this life, our brains hold an incredible amount of data, but mercifully we don't have to be aware of it all. For the most part, we consciously remember what we need to remember to function each day. The situation is similar in the spiritual world. The earthly facts that we no longer need are filed away. The quality of our life as built up through our earthly experiences is another level of memory, and this remains.

Will we be haunted by some memories we would rather forget? No, because in heaven we will live in the present, not in the past or the future. Also, as we have grown and changed, past actions that no longer reflect the person we have become will fade away. But any memory, whether active or dormant, can be accessed if there is a good use for it.

All memories that are important to who we are and what we love will stay active and vibrant. Other memories will fade into the background. They are like items in a scrapbook, carefully filed away and looked at only when there is a need or a desire for doing so. In that unique story called our Book of Life, we can enjoy all the parts that we value without being plagued by parts we would rather forget.

*"All heaven is differentiated into communities on the basis
of differences in the quality of love, and every spirit who is
raised up into heaven and becomes an angel is taken to
the community where her or his love is."*

HEAVEN AND HELL 479

CHAPTER 49

Who Are We After Death?

A person was talking to her friend: "I know that I am going to die one day. I feel healthy now, but I know that my life in this world is limited. I wonder what I will be like after death."

"That's easy," answered the friend. "You will be the same person that you are now! When you die you won't change very much."

"How can you say that? Maybe I'll be completely different."

"Some things may change, but your dominant interests and loves will not change. If they did, you wouldn't be you anymore. You would be someone else. What makes you unique is the combination of things you care about. Those interests and affections are what make you the person you are, and those do not change after death."

"Do you mean that I am stuck with my faults and imperfections?"

"No, I simply mean that the strongest loves in your heart make up who you really are. After you put off the earthly body and its imperfections, you can also put off anything that does not fit with who you really are."

"So who will I be after I die?"

"You will be yourself, only more so."

"So what kind of life is waiting for me after I die?"

"The life that is waiting for you is your life—the life you are leading here and the life you want to continue to live once you get there."

*"There is nothing natural
to which something spiritual does not answer."*

HEAVEN AND HELL 487

CHAPTER 50

Our Environment After Death

We can't help wondering what heaven looks like. The amazing thing is that people in a sense create their own environments in the spiritual world. What they see around them reflects what is going on inside them. This phenomenon is somewhat true in the natural world. Obviously we don't create mountains or sunny weather just by thinking about them, but we do create sunny moods in our hearts. Remember the cartoon where a particularly gloomy person walks around with a cloud over his head. Rain is pouring down directly on him and on no one else. There are people who create that kind of atmosphere for themselves.

Swedenborg gives examples of how the spiritual world's landscapes are shaped by the people who live there. He says that in heaven people who have had a deep love of divine truth live on mountains with their homes sparkling with precious stones. This environment surrounds them because mountains correspond to the holy, good things that lift us up close to the Lord, and because precious stones correspond to divine, true ideas from the Word.

Those who love to keep on learning and developing their minds have homes surrounded by the most beautiful gardens with plants that are constantly changing. All the various plants correspond to information, insights and intelligence that those angels love, and so they are surrounded with beautiful, ever-changing flowers, lawns and trees.

Angels who attribute everything to God have homes with lots of crystal and diamonds. Since they live a "translucent" life, acknowledging that God's goodness and truth shine through everything that they do, these angels' homes are made with translucent materials that let heavenly light through.

These examples show us why attitudes are so important. Positive attitudes create a positive environment. Negative attitudes create negative surroundings. This world is the place where we learn how to make our heaven beautiful. How do we do this? We do it by cultivating a love of God, love of other people, honesty, kindness and respect for truth. When we work on developing these positive traits, we create a beautiful world inside our own minds and begin work on creating a lovely and delightful environment for ourselves after death.

"There are three states that we pass through after
death before we arrive in either heaven or hell.
The first state is one of more outward concerns."

HEAVEN AND HELL 491

CHAPTER 51

Our Facades–The First Stage of Life in the World of Spirits

People were preparing to go to a class reunion. Some were very concerned about what they would look like and wondered what the other people would think of them after all those years. They thought a lot about what clothes to wear for each function and rehearsed the things they planned to say. They were fearful of the comparisons they expected as to who looked better, who had the best jobs, what people thought of their weight and even of the car they were driving. Of course they were very interested to see what other people would be wearing and what kind of cars they could afford.

Others were preparing for the same class reunion. They had not thought of their high school for years. They were very much wrapped up in life as it is in the present. They had been doing spiritual work, trying to rise above critical thoughts, making an effort to live in the present, looking beyond appearances to think of the deeper aspects of other people's lives. They did their packing at the last minute, simply putting in their favorite clothes, hardly even thinking about whether other people would approve or not. They thought that there was no point in trying to impress their classmates. Their purpose in going to the reunion was to be with friends, to share something of the reality of their lives and to learn something of the reality of the lives of others. Still, even these people needed to start out on a relatively surface level. In order to recognize others and to be recognized, they needed to rely on people's physical appearance. In order to initially reconnect, they might have started out talking about outer activities they do or used to do.

When people die and first enter the spiritual world, the experience can be similar to a reunion. Shortly after death people find themselves in a world much like the world they left behind. They dress in a similar way, put on similar fronts and still attach importance to outer things. This first stage is helpful, enabling them to make contact with others who may have died years before. Usually husband and wife meet, even though one may have died decades before the other. Being at first in touch with outer aspects of their lives, they can recognize each other and make some kind of contact.

Like class reunions, these meetings in the spiritual world have to begin on a fairly "surface" level, and this surface reconnection is the purpose of the first stage. Later people can move closer to their true lives. Our facades are a temporary way of dealing with others. When the facades are put off, life and relationships continue on a deeper level.

"Whatever we are like in our inward natures,
that is what we are like to eternity."

HEAVEN AND HELL 501

CHAPTER 52

Our Deeper Selves—The Second Stage of Life in the World of Spirits

Class reunions can be artificial and frustrating, but they can also be very real and fascinating. It all depends on how much the people are willing to be transparent with each other. If a reunion lasts long enough, some people get tired of the games, throw off the masks and take the risk of saying just what they mean and of doing just what they want to do. If more and more people were to do this, it could lead to some interesting changes. They might find that people they had thought of as nerds in high school were some of the people they were most drawn to now, and those who were popular in high school felt like strangers to them.

We know how tiring it can be to live behind masks and how scary it is to be open and honest. But in the long run, the masks create tremendous distance and loneliness. People who take the risk of being honest can find true bonds of understanding and love.

The same is true after death. People cannot wear masks forever. It is a wise aspect of divine providence that when we die we not only put off our material possessions and our earthly bodies; we also put off many of the pretenses of life and become more openly the people we are inside.

In the second stage of life after death, after people have become reacquainted, they want to go a little deeper. That deepening happens when they put off the facades and speak what is really on their minds and in their hearts. A husband and wife, for instance, can then see if they are deeply compatible or not. Other relationships also change as true feelings are brought out.

To some people this shift to openness is very refreshing. To finally be themselves comes as a great relief. To others this shift might be terrifying. But it must happen to all, because in the life after death we can no longer fake it. Life in the spiritual world is a truly real life, and so it is no longer possible to live life other than the way we are inside. Our true natures will come to light, and we will release all facades, habits, information and misunderstandings that are not in tune with our authentic selves. As Jesus said: "There is nothing covered that will not be revealed, and hidden that will not be known." (Matthew 10:26; compare Luke 8:17, Mark 4:22)

We can begin the process of becoming more truly ourselves even here on earth. Such a process will make our lives more real to others and to ourselves and will bring us closer to the qualities of heaven.

"Our third state after death, or the third state of our spirits, is one of instruction."

HEAVEN AND HELL 512

"After spirits have been prepared for heaven in these learning sites . . . . they are dressed in angelic clothing, usually white as linen, taken to a path that leads up toward heaven, and turned over to guardian angels there."

HEAVEN AND HELL 519

CHAPTER 53

Instruction and Orientation—The Third Stage of Life in the World of Spirits

After death, and after a person's true self has emerged during the second stage, it is time to prepare to move on to his or her new home in heaven—or, in some cases, in hell. If a person loves hellish things, then that person does not want any instruction. However, for all those who are bound for heaven, part of the preparation is learning the things they will need to know to start into their new lives.

On earth, if a person takes on a new job or enters a school for the first time, it is likely that there will be a period of orientation. The person needs to be able to get around in that new location and to understand the systems and rules that operate there. The situation is similar after death. Before arriving at their final homes in heaven, newcomers need to have a time of instruction or orientation, and this phase is the third stage of life after death.

There is one major difference between this spiritual world instruction and much of our education on earth. When I was in high school I remember the groans that went up when we tried to tackle some new problem in mathematics. "Why are we bothering to learn this? I will never have any use for this in my life." Various things were said to quell the student revolt, including the concept that such learning was teaching us how to think. This reason has validity, but the fact remains that the students who would go on in life to need and want higher mathematics for their careers or life interests would retain the information we were learning, while those who wouldn't need or use the information would not retain it.

Now imagine a Bible study group with adults looking at some part of the Scriptures. The question could be raised again: "What is the use of learning this?" On one level, learning spiritual concepts can be a good exercise, even if a person does not see a practical purpose for them yet. But the concepts that will be retained are the ones that a person feels he or she can really use in life to become a better person. The command: "Love your neighbor as yourself"(Matthew 22:39) is a principle that most people find highly practical and useful for becoming a better person.

That command is something to be incorporated into the fabric of a person's life.

When people receive instruction after death, they are taught true, spiritual concepts that they will need for the life and heavenly occupation they are heading for. The knowledge does not just go into the memory; it goes into action. Knowing the truth does not bring people into heaven, but living the truth in a useful life does. And, of course, only those who live the truth really know it.

"Our quality depends on our lives
and our lives on our loves."
HEAVEN AND HELL 521

CHAPTER 54

Why Doesn't God Just Let Us All In?

"God must be very cruel," a person said with some bitterness.

"Why is that?" was the reply.

"He is all merciful, right? Then why doesn't he use that mercy to open the gates of heaven to everyone?"

"Get serious. You remind me of the eager sophomore who kept pleading with the coach to let him play the game. Finally the coach relented and let him on the field. He was not only a hopeless player, he soon got injured because he had no idea how to protect himself. The coach finally had to explain to him that it was not merciful to let him play when he wasn't prepared and couldn't handle it. God is the same way about heaven."

"But heaven is not a football game! I would love to be in heaven. I'm ready. Send me in."

"You think you are ready, but suppose you find that you don't like it there?"

"Wait a minute. Why would anybody think that heaven wasn't nice?"

"Because they are not ready for the life of heaven. God does everything he can to prepare people for heaven and to help them love the qualities of heaven, but he does not open the gates to everyone, because he knows that some people cannot survive in heaven. They wouldn't like it and wouldn't even be able to breathe in that atmosphere."

"Are you saying that God can't MAKE people fit for heaven? He can do anything, right?"

"Well, sort of. God can do anything that follows the divine design, because God IS the divine design. And the divine design includes allowing us the freedom to choose whether to accept a life journey toward heaven or not. God knows that a way of life is only real if we choose it and if we work on it. He's merciful because he wants everyone to be in heaven and will provide us every possible opportunity to freely choose a path toward heaven. He's wise because he knows that we can only enjoy heaven if we've allowed heaven to develop inside us."

"It is not so hard to lead the life of heaven as people think, because it is simply a matter of recognizing, when something attractive comes up that we know is dishonest or unfair, that this is not to be done because it is against the divine commandments."

HEAVEN AND HELL 533

CHAPTER 55

It Is Not All That Difficult
to Get to Heaven

Two people were talking about the fact that they were both getting older and that eventually they would be leaving this world for the next.

"I am a very imperfect person. You have to be so good to get into heaven. I do not expect to be some high and wonderful angel. All I want is to squeeze in through the outer gates."

"I don't understand. It is not difficult to get into heaven. And why would you want to just squeeze in? Why not go all the way to the highest level?"

"I feel so unworthy and flawed. I am afraid I won't get into heaven at all."

"Look, we are all imperfect. That isn't the point. The point is, do you love goodness? Do you want to do the right thing? That is all it takes to get into heaven. Just try to live a good life."

"I do, I do, but I keep backsliding and making mistakes."

"So long as you regret your mistakes, you are fine. The problem is with people who prefer to make mistakes, who really want to be evil. If you want to get into heaven, all you have to do is do the best you can—believe in God and try to do what is right."

"I thought that people had to suffer and deprive themselves if they wanted to get to heaven. Some people reject worldly pleasures and eat the most basic foods. They even inflict pain on themselves to make themselves worthy of heaven."

"I can just see an angel looking down on them and saying, 'What on earth are those people on earth doing? Preparing for heaven? How do they think they can prepare for heaven by being miserable?' Heaven is a place of great joy. You don't have to do great things to get into heaven. Just live in the world, but keep an eye on heaven and try to bring God and spirituality into the things you do. Living this way is not difficult and does not require people to deprive themselves."

Hell

"All the power in the spiritual world belongs to benevolent truth and none whatsoever to malevolent falsity."

HEAVEN AND HELL 539

CHAPTER 56

Who's in Charge Down There?

It is troubling to think about hell. How could a loving God allow hell to exist? In keeping with the teaching mentioned earlier about how our life continues after death (chapter 49), dying does not change us into something we are not. Just as there are loving and good people as well as selfish and materialistic ones in the world, so also must this be true of life after death.

Rather than ask why a loving God would permit evil to exist after death, we could ask why he permits it on earth. More to the point, why does he permit both good and evil to exist in our own hearts?

The simple answer is that we have been given choice, which means that we can take any attitude we like toward life. It is more important to God that we be free than that we be good. If we weren't free to choose, we could be like good little pets, but we couldn't be humans who can truly love God and have a relationship with him. God created us to be human, and so he greatly values our ability to choose.

We are faced, then, with the prospect of heaven and hell after death. In large cities on earth, there are law-abiding citizens, and there are people with no respect for the law. It can sometimes seem that there are two cities: one governed by a duly-elected mayor and the other by some drug lord or crime boss. If this appearance were a model of the spiritual world, we might conclude that God is in charge of the good people and that Satan rules the devils. And of course that would mean that God does not have all the power. Those who go to heaven would be under God's rule, and those who go to hell would be under the control of Satan.

But the reality is that God is in charge of both heaven and hell. A more accurate analogy would be to think of a city with law-abiding citizens living freely and with those who break the law imprisoned. That set-up is certainly what most people would prefer. In that scenario, the duly-elected leader is in charge of the law-abiding citizens and also of those who have broken the law. Why permit lawless people to roam the city unchallenged? Have them confined, so that they can't continue to hurt others and so that others can have security and peace.

Even in sports we find that those who refuse to play by the rules end up in the penalty box or on the bench. They may stay there only for a time, but if they return to the game and keep breaking the rules, they get thrown out of the sport altogether. This consequence is not so much to punish them as it is to allow others to enjoy the game. There is no dominant rule breaker whom all other rule breakers must obey. The referees and umpires run the whole game, those in play and those relegated to the bench.

God rules both heaven and hell. In heaven he provides a free, productive and happy life, safe from harm. In hell he provides a place that keeps harmful people confined. There, people who have chosen an evil life are not allowed to venture out and hurt or corrupt innocent victims. By carefully governing hell, God keeps the evil from hurting the good and from hurting each other. In that way heaven is like a free city, and hell is like a prison system.

"*The Lord is constantly flowing into every individual with good, just as much into the evil person as into the good.*"

HEAVEN AND HELL 546

CHAPTER 57

People Aren't Thrown into Hell—They Jump

When I was in high school my classmate's mother was talking matter-of-factly about the shortcomings of her husband. "The trouble with old age," she said, "is that we get more and more like ourselves." As an idealistic teenager I was not expecting that kind of remark from a woman about her husband. It would not have surprised me to hear her say, "The older we get, the more angelic we become," though I knew her husband and realized that description would not fit either. After a little reflection I realized that dying and waking up in the spiritual world does not make us radically different people. Entering the afterlife allows us to become the kind of people we deep down want to be.

Since then I have wondered what kind of person I would be if I lost all fear of consequences and had all the power and wealth I wanted. Having seen in history the terrible things that have been done by people with relatively unlimited power, I realize that it is not at all obvious what we ourselves would do under those circumstances.

When we die, we find that we can do whatever we really want to do, and we have a body that cannot be destroyed. This situation could prove disastrous if we have no principles to keep ourselves behaving in a decent manner.

When I was a young man entering the army just after World War II, my family members worried about whether I had established enough principles to keep myself on the straight and narrow. I would be far from home with no reputation to preserve. Some young people can go quite wild under those circumstances. Fortunately for me, I was not attracted to any dens of iniquity I might have met along the way.

Reading in the book *Heaven and Hell*, I learned that the Lord does not cast anyone into hell. Those who are deeply wicked dive in headfirst. They've filled their hearts with destructive pleasures, and so they head directly for the place they will feel at home—a place where people love to hurt and control each other. They are not being punished by an angry god. They are simply following their instincts and lusts.

When evil people get to hell, they soon find that they cannot do all the things they want to do. Those who have been cruel dictators in the world might find themselves confronted with people who are more powerful and cruel than themselves, tyrants who will not tolerate competition. Those who have been thieves find that they experience severe pain whenever they take something that is not theirs. There are limitations in hell, because in a place where everyone wants to be the top boss and have all the possessions, no one can have their way. It simply doesn't work.

Just as a brick wall is not angry with the person who keeps banging his or her fist against it, there is no anger in the system of punishment, just painful consequences. In this way people in hell arrive at a place where they can fantasize all manner of evil deeds, but the moment they do such deeds, they suffer dire consequences.

God is pure love and therefore out of mercy will allow people to live where they want to live in the spiritual world. Though it greatly saddens God that people would choose to live in a place of hatred, it is the home that those people have made for themselves, and they really cannot live anywhere else.

However, a loving God cannot permit even those in hell to do the kind of destructive harm to each other that they would wish to do, and when they set out to do violence against each other, they are stopped. Therefore, though hell is the preferred life for those who live there, existence there is filled with frustration. What a contrast to the life of heaven, where angels can do whatever they want, because what they want is always for the sake of loving and helping others.

Why would people choose to live the way that they do in hell? At some point they became caught up in destructive pleasures and then kept cultivating these pleasures until there was little or no room left for goodness. I have seen people whose outward lives seemed to follow that pattern. If those people have developed a love for that way of life, and if they don't take advantage of the many chances to change, I can see that such people might continue to live that pattern as their chosen existence after death.

"Spirits move spontaneously toward kindred spirits because they are motivated by what attracts and delights them."

HEAVEN AND HELL 552

CHAPTER 58

People in the Hells Are Absorbed in Evils Because of Their Selfishness and Worldliness

In many movies it is easy to tell the good guys from the bad guys. The good guys are pleasant-looking. The bad guys have ugly sneers on their faces. I have sometimes wondered how the actors manage to communicate this evil quality. I imagine them getting into a frame of mind where they hold everyone else in contempt and think only of how everything relates to them. In order to play the part, these actors conjure up emotions of cynicism, cruelty, vengefulness and deceit.

Some philosophers have wondered if there is really such a thing as "evil" in the world. Suppose we substitute the word "harmful." Are there people on this planet who are toxic and destructive of the happiness of others? Simply watching the daily news or reading history shows plenty of evidence of such people.

And what is at the heart of evil? Is it not making oneself the center of the universe and wanting all other people to be subservient? Is it not being devoid of any concern for the common welfare? We think of the mad scientist who wants to destroy the world. Any appeal to mercy or compassion is quite useless. Such totally self-centered people cannot have relationships with others, because they think of others only as enemies or slaves, not as beings of equal importance to themselves.

The monstrous people portrayed in our entertainment are for the most part extreme caricatures. The challenge for us is to see the part of ourselves that is completely self-focused, and, having seen it, to refuse to let that part of us dominate our lives. The only real cure is to be lifted up to experience the unselfish love of God and allow that love to shape our lives.

This evil self-love is not at all the same as what has been called "loving yourself" or "self-respect." Many people suffer from not loving themselves enough. It is good to accept ourselves on all levels. But we must beware of making this love of self the most important thing in our lives. That kind of self-centeredness leads to all manner of evil and falsity.

The other corrupting force in human nature is worldliness, or making material things more important than heavenly ones. Here again we see in the daily news and in history how destructive the unbridled love of money can be.

People in hell have become completely absorbed in the destructive forms of selfishness and worldliness. So how can we rise above these tendencies in ourselves that would, if unchecked, draw us into hell? The simple answer to both evils is to have some cause in your heart that is more important than your ego and to value the things of the spirit above the riches of the world.

"Because hellfire is love for oneself and the
world, it is also all the craving of those loves,
since craving is love reaching out."

HEAVEN AND HELL 570

CHAPTER 59

Hellfire

Anger may be a healthy response to injury, or to a threat to yourself or people and causes that you love. But even so anger eats away at you and makes your life very uncomfortable. People who constantly seethe with anger are very unhappy people. One of our great challenges in life is to learn to deal with anger. We can acknowledge that anger is in us. We can take steps to right the wrong that has stimulated the anger. Eventually we have to let the anger go. Otherwise it will eat us up. People are not punished for their anger. Rather they are punished *by* their anger, just as they are not punished *for* putting their hand in the fire but are punished *by* putting their hand in the fire.

The Bible talks about hellfire, and some people think that the flames of that fire come from a vengeful god. Some preachers even yell at their congregations warning them against the wrath of God. This method may help some congregation members to lead better lives, though I doubt it. But such an approach is taken at the cost of making God into a dreadful tyrant, an all-powerful being who delights in inflicting pain on evil-doers.

Since the life after death is a spiritual condition, not a physical one, hellfire must have something to do with the spirit, not the body. Those in hell are not scorched by some kind of physical fire that attacks them from outside of themselves. The fires of hell are all an inside job brought on by the lust, greed, hatred and malevolence that burn within the people there.

People still living on earth can get caught up in this spiritual hellfire. It might seem to them that they have no choice but to seethe with hatred against criminals, burn with lust for certain alluring people of the opposite sex, or get all fired up at the thought of fabulous wealth, but they do have a choice. It is a matter of deep spiritual work to recognize the destructive nature of this hellfire, to refrain from fanning these infernal flames in ourselves, and to take steps to live instead with forgiveness, true love and contentment with our lot in life.

"Just as angelic spirits think and intend and speak and act from their good, so hellish spirits do the same from their evil."

HEAVEN AND HELL 577

CHAPTER 60

The Malice and Craft of Hellish Spirits

A bully was beating up a younger boy. The younger boy was too small to do much damage, but he fought back bravely. The fight was getting really ugly when an adult intervened, separated the two combatants, and said to the younger boy: "I know he didn't really want to hurt you." That might have been a kind thing to say. It just didn't happen to be true. Not only did the bully want to hurt the younger child, but he also took great delight in cruelty. He often picked on children younger and weaker than himself and especially enjoyed it when the children screamed in pain.

It is hard to imagine that people can take sadistic pleasure in hurting others. I can hardly believe, for example, that there are computer nerds who seem to take delight in creating viruses that wreak havoc in computers all over the world. The sad fact is that some people delight in doing evil.

When I was a teenager we were all shocked when our high school building caught fire. We were even more amazed to learn that someone had deliberately set fire to the building and that afterward he was the person on the main road directing traffic! Why did he do it? Evidently he loved making buildings burn and possibly didn't even mind if the destruction involved killing people inside.

Swedenborg reports that people who were maliciously evil on earth continue to be that way after death and with even greater venom and skill. People are given their whole earthly lives to repent and change. They are even given time in the world of spirits in the first stages after death if the evil behavior was a result of severe misunderstandings or imbalances that made a person unable to freely choose to change. With these chances it's possible that some very nasty people may, with difficulty, repent and change, but others remain addicted to violence and don't want to change.

We do well to protect ourselves against the insidious workings of evil. Our protection comes from looking to the Lord for help and living the best kind of life we can live. In this way we stay in touch with the tremendous power of divine love, which can drive back a whole army of evil spirits with just a glance.

"The heavens . . . are on the higher ground, the world of spirits . . . is in the lower areas, and beneath both lie the hells."

HEAVEN AND HELL 583

Chapter 61

What Hell Looks Like

The house lights dim. The audience is hushed. The curtain opens to reveal a scene of great splendor. The people on the stage are dressed in elegant clothes and are having a conversation in a lavishly-decorated dining room. At first it seems as if they might love each other, but they are speaking very harshly, and their faces are contorted with anger and greed.

As the story unfolds, the audience finds that the man in the story has recently come into great wealth. He left his wife to set himself up in this luxurious home, and he has been having a whole series of relationships with women who are beautiful to look at but have no interest in him as a person.

He finds he is restless, wanting more and more. He has no real friends, just a parade of people trying to get money from him.

Gradually the light changes to reveal the fact that the people are not beautiful at all. Their faces are ugly, and their clothes are filthy rags. The dining room is not a room at all, but a dark cave full of bones and garbage.

This scene provides a glimpse into the reality of evil and of hell. Those in hell do not think of themselves as living in squalor, because the light is too dim, and they are too full of themselves to even notice. They might think they are in heaven.

Since both heaven and hell are not places but states of mind, the scenery is simply a reflection of what is going on inside the people. If they are ignorant or absorbed in false ideas, their surroundings are very dim. If their hearts are full of hatred, their surroundings are fiery. If they constantly create lies to hide the reality of their intentions, their atmosphere is black with smoke.

"Everything in the heavens and the hells is so arranged that each individual there is in a personal equilibrium."

HEAVEN AND HELL 594

CHAPTER 62

The Equilibrium Between Heaven and Hell

It is easy to see how two things that are roughly equal can balance each other, like two people of similar weight on a see-saw. Two unequal people can also balance each other on a see-saw, regardless of the difference in their weights, provided the arms of the seesaw are long enough. A tiny child can exert as much downward pressure as a huge adult, if the child is at the far end of the seesaw and the adult is near the middle. Equilibrium can be achieved between things that are somewhat different. There can also be a balance between two things that are enormously different, like the light of a single candle and the sun. The light of a candle a quarter of an inch behind a piece of paper will outshine the sun 93 million miles away.

These examples help to show how two things as different as the power of good and the power of evil can be balanced. Good and evil are very different. In absolute terms good has all the power, but evil can exert great pressure when it is near to us and when we think that it is good.

Equilibrium in nature also involves forces. Newton's third law of motion states that for every action there is an equal and opposite reaction. When some force in nature pushes one way, some other force pushes back. This way, things don't constantly collapse under the pressure of a force. The fact that there is always another force pushing back keeps things in balance and allows us to move in whatever direction we want. There is no one force requiring us to move in only one direction.

Spiritually, God keeps things in equilibrium between good and evil so that we are free to choose which direction we want to go. In order to maintain this spiritual equilibrium, there has to be a spiritual equivalent to Newton's third law of motion. When a force of good moves one way, there has to be a reaction from the opposite force of evil, and vice versa. Otherwise we would have no choice about what direction to move.

Just as there is a great difference between good and evil, there is also a vast difference between truth and falsity, so much so that we can't help wondering how they could ever be in balance. The answer is that the real power lies in the truth, but falsity exerts force when it is very near us and presents itself as the truth. Also, when truth flows into us, there is a reaction from the force of falsity, so doubts easily crop up when we're considering true ideas.

We are subject to doubt throughout our lives. We long to know the truth. At times we seem to find it, but because of the law of equilibrium, falsity pushes back and tries to convince us that false ideas are true. At times truth and falsity even seem to be equal. This appearance forces us to struggle with issues, to search for the truth and to pray for enlightenment. The struggle is not always enjoyable, and yet it causes us to really work to make true ideas our own, freely chosen.

We human beings are set in a spiritual equilibrium between good and evil, between truth and falsity. Because of this equilibrium, we have the freedom and the ability to tip the scales in any direction we want.

"Nothing becomes part of us except as a result of some affection of love. . . This is why we cannot be reformed except in a state of freedom."

HEAVEN AND HELL 598

CHAPTER 63

Our Freedom Depends on the Balance Between Heaven and Hell

A young man was making a spiritual choice. He never would have labeled it as such at the time, but that is what it was.

He had been mistreated by a young woman he had wanted to date. He felt anger and a desire for revenge. He fantasized about how he could humiliate her and make her suffer. His mind raced with all the arguments he could make against her—wild, crazy thoughts which seemed perfectly logical to him at the time. In his imagination he was a skillful lawyer, creating a case against the woman, in which he gave the most damaging arguments against her and pleaded for the worst possible punishment. He noticed how delicious these scenes all seemed, almost to the point that he was glad to have had such an obvious injustice done to him, since it gave full reign to his sense of martyrdom in having been treated so cruelly.

He did not see the girl again for a long time, during which his thoughts began to vacillate between the sweet thoughts of revenge and a gentler line of thinking that included some reflection on his own inadequacies.

At one point he began to feel horror at his own viciousness, realizing that the girl was not the cause of his violent reaction. It was painful for him to admit to himself that the incident had brought out a mean side of his character that he had not seen before. The picture he had of himself as a really nice and kind person was getting ragged at the edges. He saw the ugliness of his lower self and was ashamed that he had allowed it to run his imagination for so long.

He began to get in touch with a more balanced and kind side of his personality. He remembered those cartoons with an angel sitting and smiling on one shoulder of a person and a devil smirking and threatening on the other shoulder. Yes, he was familiar with these two characters. Now he realized that he stood balanced between them. He could go one way or the other. If he went with his diabolical side, he could conjure up endless excuses and reasons for doing so. If he went with the shining angel, he could see all of the wisdom that supported that view.

The man was then struck very forcibly by an important concept: "I have a choice! This choice is what determines my life! I have seen both the evil and the good in myself. I am not a victim. And when I choose, it is a choice about *my* life—not the life of my parents or my friends. My experience is the life I have chosen. I have the ability to intend either good or evil and to think either truth or falsity. I can opt for one instead of the other. This choice is my freedom and my life. Thank God I can choose heaven or hell!"

*"The soul is nothing more nor less than our life,
while the spirit is the actual person, and the body is an
earthly thing we carry around in the world."*

HEAVEN AND HELL 602

Conclusion

The book *Heaven and Hell*, as the title indicates, ends with a discussion of hell. Hell is an unpleasant subject, but the unpleasantness is mitigated by these important points:

1. Hell is not a punishment. Hell is simply a state of mind experienced by people who are selfish and worldly.

2. People are not cast into hell. They choose it.

3. By understanding some concepts about hell, we can notice when we are in hellish moods, and we can take steps to get out of them into a more positive state of mind.

There are many wonderful ideas in *Heaven and Hell*, but still the book cannot possibly tell us all there is to know about the life beyond the grave. No doubt when we pass through the barrier we call death, we are in for many surprises.

The ideas presented in *Heaven and Hell*, though written centuries ago, can certainly resonate with us today. These ideas ring true, I believe, because they help us to understand our own inner spiritual world, giving insights into the depth and complexities of our own human nature. The ideas in *Heaven and Hell* can also inspire us to make the kind of choices that lead to greater peace of mind and increased effectiveness in our desire to make our lives a gift to others. And when we've developed this heaven inside us, we will find ourselves living in the beauty of heaven after death.

References

Swedenborg, Emanuel, *Arcana Caelestia*. (Third Latin edition) London, England: Swedenborg Society (1973)

Holy Bible: The New King James Version. Nashville, TN: Thomas Nelson Publishers, 1982.

Moody, Raymond A., Jr. *Life After Life: the Investigation of a Phenomenon — Survival of Bodily Death*. New York: Bantam Books, 1975.

Skeat, Walter W. *A Concise Etymological Dictionary of the English Language*. Oxford: Oxford University Press, 1951.

Swedenborg, Emanuel, *Heaven and Hell*. West Chester, PA: Swedenborg Foundation, 2000. Translation by George F. Dole

Endnotes

[1]Shakespeare, William, *As You Like It*, act 2, scene 1, lines 15-18. New York: Penguin Putnam, 1963. Edited by Albert Gilman.

[2]Psychiatrist Wilson Van Dusen (1923-2005) worked with people who hear voices, and he wrote about his experience. Van Dusen distinguishes two different kinds of spirits—what he calls the higher and lower orders, which might also be called angelic or infernal spirits:

> In my dialogues with patients, I learned of two orders of experience, borrowing from the voices themselves, called the higher and the lower order. Lower order voices are similar to drunks at a bar who like to tease and torment just for the fun of it . . . . The higher order is much more likely to be symbolic, religious, supportive, genuinely instructive; it can communicate directly with the inner feelings of the patient. (Van Dusen, Wilson, *The Presence of Other Worlds*. West Chester, PA: Swedenborg Foundation, 2004. From a chapter entitled: "The Presence of Spirits in Madness.")

[3]www.westsidestory.com/lyrics: "One Hand, One Heart" lyrics by Stephen Sondheim. © 1956, 1957 Amberson Holdings LLC and Stephen Sondheim. Copyright renewed. Leonard Bernstein Music Publishing Company LLC, Publisher.

About the Author

Frank S. Rose was born in 1927 in Bryn Athyn, Pennsylvania, the ninth child of Don and Marjorie Rose. Frank began painting in his teens. He graduated from the Bryn Athyn Theological School in 1952 and then served for 51 years as an ordained clergyman in Europe, Canada and the United States, doing painting on the side. Frank and his wife Louise moved to Tucson, Arizona in 1982 where he served as pastor of Sunrise Chapel until his retirement in 2003. He is a past president of the Southern Arizona Watercolor Guild and a member of the Arizona Native Plant Society. Since his retirement he has devoted himself to art and photography, combining it with an interest in botany, and also to writing. For many years his artwork was available in Tucson from El Presidio Gallery.

Also by Frank S. Rose:

Reflections on Providence
(Fountain Publishing)

Purp Climbs the Tallest Tree in the World
(Fountain Publishing)

Mountain Wildflowers of Southern Arizona: A Field Guide to the Santa Catalina Mountains and Other Nearby Ranges
(Sonoran Desert Museum)

More copies of *Reflections on Heaven and Hell* are available from Fountain Publishing at www.fountainpublishing.com.

Heaven and Hell
**by Emanuel Swedenborg
is available from
the Swedenborg Foundation at www.swedenborg.com.**

**Both are available at
the New Church Bookstore at
http://store.newchurch.org.**